Developing an Outstanding Curriculum

Our role as educators is to develop a curriculum which facilitates outstanding learning and which builds social, cultural, and educational capital. The curriculum is much more than a content-driven document, it is the vehicle for educational change. This book complements the *Make it Outstanding Series* and is central to subject development. It has a strong focus on combining curriculum theory and translating this to a practical approach schools can adapt and implement with ease.

Packed full of practical strategies and examples to facilitate curriculum conversations within subject and senior leadership teams, the chapters provide a considered balance between theory and application. Supporting teachers, curriculum leaders, senior leaders, and headteachers in leading and implementing the curriculum within their schools, the book covers:

- An overview of different curriculum models
- How to develop the curriculum intent from the whole school vision
- Developing the composite and component structure
- How we implement the curriculum with a focus on learning episodes
- How we assess the curriculum
- Social, cultural, and educational capital
- How we quality assure the curriculum

Developing an Outstanding Curriculum is an essential read for all teachers, curriculum leaders, senior leaders, and headteachers who want to ensure that they drive the development of an outstanding curriculum.

Jayne Bartlett is Headteacher, author of *Becoming an Outstanding Mathematics Teacher, Outstanding Differentiation for Learning and Outstanding Assessment for Learning*, and series editor of the *Make it Outstanding Series*. She has worked for over 20 years in the education sector with a focus on curriculum and teaching and learning; ensuring that we provide opportunities for all students to succeed. She is passionate about capital in education. She invited Emma Housden, who has worked with her for three years, to contribute to authoring this book.

Emma Housden has worked in education for 11 years and has progressed from a teacher of mathematics to Deputy Headteacher overseeing all aspects of curriculum development.

Becoming an Outstanding Teacher
Series Editor: Jayne Bartlett

Becoming an Outstanding Mathematics Teacher
Jayne Bartlett

Becoming an Outstanding English Teacher
Kate Sida-Nicholls

Becoming an Outstanding Geography Teacher
Mark Harris

Becoming an Outstanding History Teacher
Sally Thorne

Becoming an Outstanding Languages Teacher, 2nd Edition
Steve Smith

Becoming an Outstanding Music Teacher
Martin Leigh

Developing an Outstanding Curriculum
Jayne Bartlett with contributions from Emma Housden

For a full list of titles see: https://www.routledge.com/Becoming-an-Outstanding-Teacher/book-series/BARTLETT

Developing an Outstanding Curriculum

Jayne Bartlett
with contributions from
Emma Housden

LONDON AND NEW YORK

Designed cover image: © Getty Images

First published 2024
by Routledge
4 Park Square, Milton Park, Abingdon, Oxon OX14 4RN

and by Routledge
605 Third Avenue, New York, NY 10158

Routledge is an imprint of the Taylor & Francis Group, an informa business

© 2024 Jayne Bartlett and Emma Housden

The right of Jayne Bartlett and Emma Housden to be identified as authors of this work has been asserted in accordance with sections 77 and 78 of the Copyright, Designs and Patents Act 1988.

All rights reserved. No part of this book may be reprinted or reproduced or utilised in any form or by any electronic, mechanical, or other means, now known or hereafter invented, including photocopying and recording, or in any information storage or retrieval system, without permission in writing from the publishers.

Trademark notice: Product or corporate names may be trademarks or registered trademarks, and are used only for identification and explanation without intent to infringe.

British Library Cataloguing-in-Publication Data
A catalogue record for this book is available from the British Library

ISBN: 9781032287317 (hbk)
ISBN: 9781032287324 (pbk)
ISBN: 9781003298274 (ebk)

DOI: 10.4324/9781003298274

Typeset in Melior
by Newgen Publishing UK

For Dad, Oliver, Olivia, Darren, David, Coco and Keith and in loving memory of my inspirational Mom who I loved dearly, miss every single day and whose loss reminds us how precious life is. I love you Mom. Thank you all for always believing in me. Jayne Bartlett

Contents

	Acknowledgements	ix
	Introduction	1
1	Introducing the curriculum	4
2	Understanding and developing the composite and component model	15
3	Identifying curriculum knowledge	29
4	The learning cycle	45
5	Assessing the curriculum	83
6	Social, cultural, and educational capital	101
7	Quality assurance of the curriculum	117
	Conclusion	129
Bibliography		135
Index		139

Acknowledgements

This book forms the culmination of work on the curriculum, an area I am incredibly passionate about and whilst written last is probably the central reference for the *Make it Outstanding Series* and I thank the team at Routledge once again for providing another fantastic opportunity. I invited Emma Housden, a talented Deputy Headteacher who has worked with me for the past three years, to contribute to the authoring of this book.

Most importantly, I have to thank my family for all of their support and patience whilst I was writing this book. This one has had to be squeezed in with the busyness of life, running an amazing school and balancing just living! It's been a very challenging few years for us all and life as always has ups and downs, but my family remain the most important thing to me. My most amazing dad, thank you, I don't know what I'd ever do without your words of wisdom and support, always looking after everyone else. Oliver and Olivia, you are incredible and are talented in everything that you do, I am so very fortunate to have two amazing children and I am so proud of you both. Darren, for all the things you do to help and support, for your artistic skills and of course for supplying endless cups of tea. David, my brother, for always having kept things constant. Coco (our adorable cat), for her continual attempts to sit on my laptop whilst writing this book (and deleting parts!) and Keith (our cheeky pony) who keeps me away from the computer and provides lots of entertainment. Thank you all, my most amazing family.

Finally, I hope you find this an interesting and useful read, a book that you can dip in and out of for ideas. Most important I hope that this book ignites meaningful conversations within your schools.

Jayne Bartlett

Acknowledgements

Firstly, I would like to thank Jayne for inviting me to work on this amazing project. Reliving the journey of developing the curriculum has made me proud of the work we did as a school.

Secondly, I want to show gratitude to my family and in particular my parents for always being there for me and for encouraging me throughout my life. Thank you for believing in me.

Last but not least, I would like to thank William. He has supported me throughout this whole process, cooked me countless meals, did the majority of the cleaning and most importantly for going on numerous long runs so I can get some peace and quiet.

Emma Housden

Introduction

Everything we do as educationalists draws back to the curriculum. Put simply: the curriculum is at the heart of a school. Knowledge is at the heart of the curriculum. A school is at the heart of knowledge.

An outstanding curriculum builds social, cultural, and educational capital and is our vehicle to developing learner knowledge. Our role as educators is to develop the individual as a whole and the curriculum is at the core. This book combines curriculum and cognitive theory with lots of practical examples. It will support educationalists at all levels, teachers, curriculum leaders, senior leaders, and headteachers in leading and implementing the curriculum within their schools. Each chapter ends with a checklist of questions to prompt discussion.

In Chapter 1 we look at what we mean by the curriculum and explore the different curriculum models including the spiral curriculum and the network curriculum. We develop the reader's understanding of powerful curriculum ideas and the progressive model, providing them with an understanding of the key concepts that will allow them to select the best curriculum model to drive impact in each subject area. A core focus of this chapter is that to create an outstanding curriculum, the curriculum must be at the heart of everything we do as educationalists. We introduce the over-arching structure of the curriculum, from the intent to the composite and component model, allowing leaders to identify key principles aligned with their school values.

The curriculum intent is discussed in Chapter 2, developing subject intent from the whole school curriculum intent. The whole school intent should be linked to the school values and ethos, and we guide leaders on how to ensure that this is an integral part of their intent statement. This whole school intent then acts as an umbrella for each subject. At subject level we focus on how we identify what we want students to learn and by key points in their educational journey. We develop an understanding of linking and sequencing the

Introduction

curriculum to ensure that leaders are able to maximize their curriculum impact and ensure that students' knowledge is built upon progressively with a clear understanding of inter-connectivity. This is explored through the composite and component model.

Knowledge is at the heart of the curriculum and the curriculum is a vehicle for imparting knowledge. Yet teachers and leaders often find pinpointing the specific knowledge the most challenging. How do we select what students will learn or indeed will not learn? National curriculum provide educators with a guide, underpinning the aim of creating a school-level curriculum that is at least as ambitions, but the skill for leaders is to be able to select the most appropriate knowledge to achieve a progressive and well-balanced curriculum, knowing how to select what students will learn and what they will not learn. In Chapter 3 we explore the different types of knowledge, how to select what students will learn. This chapter looks at the in-depth development of a composite with a focus on developing clear rationale for the specific knowledge and how this will be broken down into components. We look in detail at component level and how to identify the subject-specific knowledge and core vocabulary. The component is where we are forensic about the learning and scaffolding and challenge are key features that need to be understood. Often scaffolding is mistaken for low-level support and this is most certainly not the case. It is essential that teachers understand that there are core end points that all students need to reach. We explore a range of examples across different subjects through the development phase.

In Chapter 4 we focus on the learning cycle and how we implement the curriculum through our lessons. The lesson is the key driver for knowledge and having a strong understanding of the learning cycle will ensure that the curriculum is well implemented. This chapter explores the importance of knowledge retrieval, assessment for learning, independence in learning, and how we draw our learning to a close. Here we explore further the delivery of effective scaffolding and challenge and the pedagogical context of the curriculum.

Central to any curriculum is high-quality assessment. In Chapter 5 we explore the role of assessment and introduce the interim and end of composite assessment. Both types of assessment are a critical component to the success of a curriculum, and we explore how to ensure that your assessment assesses the curriculum knowledge and how each question is able to link to a specific point of knowledge and a specific component within the curriculum. Assessment itself, however, is pointless unless we do something with the outcome of the assessment, and this must be at an individual student level. Here we introduce the concept of meaningful re-teach and curriculum review. Curriculum review must be at all levels from student to Headteacher for a highly effective and outstanding curriculum.

The curriculum as a learning tool is more than simply 'what students will know'. It provides a much richer and deeper experience through the development of social and cultural capital which runs parallel to our educational capital. How we develop our learners is a central part of creating an outstanding curriculum and in Chapter 6 we explore what we mean by each form of capital and how we can gain meaningful integration at all levels. This chapter explores the role of personal development and how personal development is integral to curriculum success.

The curriculum must be at the heart of everything we do as educationalists. It is a living entity that we must ensure we quality assure at all levels. Chapter 7 explores all levels of quality assurance focusing on leadership and management with quality assurance through: the class teacher, the department team, the curriculum leaders, senior leadership to the Headteacher. For the curriculum to really drive change we must have accountability at all levels and in this chapter we provide lots of examples of how to ensure a robust quality assurance of the curriculum.

The book concludes with a checklist of guidance on key elements of curriculum construction, providing discussion points at a curriculum and whole school level. It allows the reader to have a very simple and structured approach to their curriculum development and a checklist to ensure that they are supported at all levels.

Chapter 1

Introducing the curriculum

Most countries have a national curriculum; an intended curriculum which schools translate and implement at classroom level. National curriculum are typically lists of content that tell us 'what' students should know. They cover the content from early years through to the final years of statutory study. What national curriculum do not tell us is 'how' students will learn. How students learn is influenced by the choice of curriculum model which translates the national curriculum to the implemented curriculum. There are different curriculum models which we will explore in this chapter, but the fundamental principle remains the same and our role is to ensure students learn what we want them to know. To facilitate this, we must also be able to clearly identify what we do *not* want students to know, and careful consideration should be given to this process during the planning phase.

The term 'broad and balanced' is frequently used and this means that we ensure students receive a well-rounded diet of curriculum subjects so that they develop, for example, their creativity through art, drama, music as much as the more traditional subjects of maths, English, and science. A broad and balanced curriculum develops students' skills, knowledge, and understanding across a wide range of subject disciplines and each subject reinforces the development in the other subject, whether directly or indirectly. Reading, for instance, a play in English is far easier to contextualize if students have studied drama. We must acknowledge that to create this is not possible without innovation. While we want to develop our students' interest in each subject, we must recognize there is a vast array (infinite array) of subject knowledge, and it is the 'what' we want students to know that should have significant investment. The breadth is how much of the subject domain our students will experience. We must be careful that we select the most appropriate knowledge within our curriculum to allow depth but equally that we don't narrow this to the focus of an examination curriculum.

To maximize efficacy of our curriculum we must therefore ensure we pinpoint the knowledge and that it is then well planned, appropriate, and coherent. Well-planned links to our curriculum sequencing and the horizontal and vertical progression which creates a complex map of learning. Horizontal progression refers to development across an academic year and is where ideas and knowledge domains are connected. Vertical progression refers to the development through subsequent years and can involve developing a concept in increasing complexity as topics are revisited. For example, in mathematics if we take the basic concept of 'solving equations' we may develop the underlying process of balancing and the concept of the equals sign, through for example $2 + 3 = 5$ (which underpins all processes) in the early years of a student's education. As they reach for example age 11, we may begin to progress though to solving simple equations, such as, $3x + 7 = 35$. This may develop to more complex problems which draw from a combination of, for example, algebra and shape and space. It is a vertical progression but with clear links as we travel through the curriculum to ensure that students do not see these as a series of discrete and unconnected 'topics'. We should note that this refers to vertical progression within a specific subject, but vertical progression also refers to the development of coherence through the wider curriculum across subjects. This is a much more complicated web and one that we have yet to see mastered.

Coherence means ensuring that when we look across our curriculum structure that the learning allows connections to be made at the most appropriate time and this reinforces memory and application. For example, if we are studying Victorian England in history and Oliver Twist in English literature, then does our curriculum ensure we do this at the most coherent time or is there limited or no communication between our subject curricula? Coherence allows students to make connections and will ultimately impact positively on student learning. It is much more than 'cross curricular' opportunities which we often see schools attempt to highlight on curriculum documents. This is not simply about highlighting links, for example, mathematical opportunities in physics, such as the use of scatter graphs, but looking at the 'how', 'when', and 'why' to allow coherence of implementation and of application. When do we teach scatter graphs in mathematics? How do we teach it? Why are we teaching it, how we are, and when we do? How do we use the application in science to support the implementation in mathematics and how do we use the implementation in mathematics to support the application in science?

We must also address how culturally rich our curriculum is and in Chapter 6 we explore this in detail. How does the content we have selected align with cultural development and what is valuable for our students to know? These thought processes should be embedded into every layer of curriculum development.

The school vision

The school vision outlines our purpose and is brought to life through our mission statement and will be embedded into the whole school curriculum intent.

- Vision statement: where the school aspires to go; these are often concise statements which provide direction.

- Mission statement: defines how the vision will be achieved; 'who' we are and 'what' we value by providing priorities and focus.

- Values: how must we 'behave' to achieve our vision; a collective culture.

Put simply the vision describes where we hope to be if our mission is fulfilled. Combined with the school values this forms the basis of the strategic plan which formulates the actions we will take to achieve our vision through clear objectives, success criteria and evaluation of impact. This interconnectedness is illustrated in Figure 1.1.

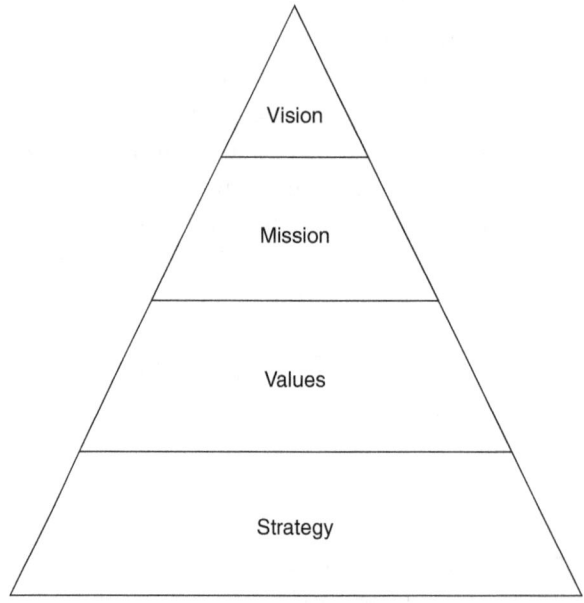

Figure 1.1 Vision, mission, values and strategy

A subject vision is developed in much the same way but will carefully align with the whole school vision and should be ambitious and clearly understood by the subject team. It needs to be inspirational but must be relevant. This point is often overlooked but a vision which is not relevant to the context and tailored to the school will not have impact. The vision feeds into the subject intent statement and the purpose of studying the subject, the 'why'. The subject strategic plan will be the vehicle to bring the vision to life.

Key questions to work through with your team when developing the vision and mission:

- What is truly inspiring about our subject?
- How will it feed into the wider world?
- Why do students study your subject?
- What key skills will students develop?
- How does our subject support other areas of the curriculum?

These questions are only very simple prompts, and it is essential that your vision and mission are clearly communicated and understood by all. Too often we see these on the top of subject strategic plans and then filed or revisited on occasion, usually when the quality assurance cycle dictates. If this is the case for you then you are not walking your vision, resourcing it, supporting it or measuring it. It should be something that you live and breathe as a team each day and against which you measure your impact and progress. Each objective in your subject strategic plan contributes to achieving the vision and therefore by measuring the impact of our strategic plan through carefully crafted success criteria we will be measuring how well we are working towards achieving our vision. Everything should link and we liken this to the silver thread.

Values are an agreement of a collective set of behaviours that we all exhibit to deliver the vision. For example, if aspiration is a value in your school, then how is aspiration for all students built into your curriculum model? If resilience is one of your values, then how do you ensure the curriculum builds the resilient learner; do they know how to fail? Do they understand the importance of 'trying' and 'not giving up'? Do they understand the concept of the critical friend? Whatever our school values, they must align and be the behaviours that all stakeholders buy into and model to bring the vision to life. We must ensure that the values we determine are suitable vehicles to realize the vision.

Different types of curriculum model

There are different types of curriculum model and here we will discuss the spiral curriculum and the network curriculum. The spiral curriculum is based on cognitive theory and was developed by Bruner in 1960. It bases curriculum development in an upward trajectory which revisits prior learning and builds upon it. The spiral curriculum has both horizontal and vertical integration. Mastery is achieved as key concepts are built upon and revisited in different contexts with a strong focus on connectivity. It works well for science and mathematical subjects where there are relatively well-mapped knowledge domains. Sequencing is obviously critical to the success of this curriculum and when students re-visit a topic, they develop their expertise and their memory. Knowledge develops from a basic understanding to a more advanced level.

Bruner states that 'any subject can be taught effectively in some intellectually honest form to any child at any stage of development' (Bruner, 1960). The spiral curriculum needs to be balanced with the rate that we introduce new material or that we re-visit material as this can lead to students not having sufficient time to master the content. This can lead to superficial learning when compared to deeper learning where we spend a greater period developing the concepts or knowledge.

Non-linear curriculum models such as the network or web model are an alternative to the spiral curriculum and tend to be favoured by art subjects. In part this is because in these subjects, learning objectives are not necessarily as easily identifiable as linear. Students develop their knowledge in different concepts and by application. An example of how this has developed is the lattice model developed by Efland (1995). Students develop their transfer skills when they can make connections between different topics. There is a danger, however, that the content can be too complex too soon and that there are no limits on the horizontal development.

The key to the choice of curriculum model that you use as a base is to ensure it is well researched and ultimately a combination of the two models, blended to suit the subject needs will most likely give the best framework. No school wants to take a rigid approach, we want to re-visit learning and develop depth as we progress, but we also want to dedicate appropriate time to different 'topics' and we want to allow students the opportunity to make connections between concepts and link their learning. Mapping out your own approach will facilitate curriculum conversations.

Developing the curriculum intent

The curriculum is a vehicle for delivering the vision. Each principle or pillar acts as a 'theme' which should support implementation across all subjects. The first step is to identify each principle; these should be aligned to the school values.

Pillars of the curriculum may be based, for example, on: literacy, numeracy, assessment for learning, independence, research. We would recommend no more than five pillars to ensure that the curriculum remains focused. They should be linked to the context of your school and the most meaningful tend to be developed with stakeholder input. This can be visualized through Figure 1.2.

In recent years there has been a move towards curriculum development coupled with an understanding of cognitive science and memory. A curriculum which tells us 'what' to learn is of limited value if it is not combined with powerful thought behind 'how' we learn coupled with the skilful selection and sequencing of knowledge, defined as the curriculum knowledge.

How we select our curriculum knowledge underpins learning. The starting point is typically driven by a national curriculum framework, such as, The National Curriculum in England (National Curriculum, 2018) which outlines the content from key stage 1 (KS1; age 5 to 7) to key stage 4 (KS4; age 15 to 16). These frameworks provide us with the content knowledge, for example, at key

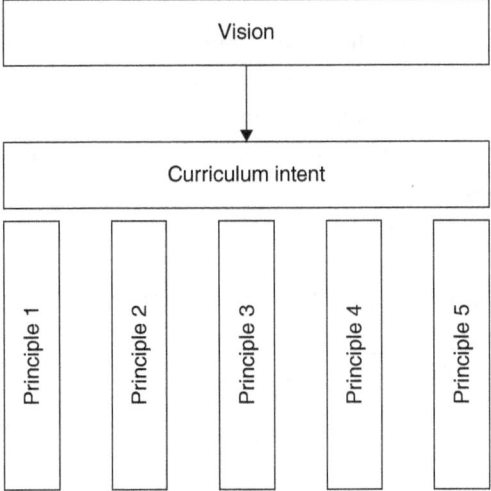

Figure 1.2 Curriculum structural design

stage 3 (KS3; age 11 to 14) a knowledge point in biology is, 'the similarities and differences between plant and animal cells' (National Curriculum, 2018, p. 158).

Subject teams should determine the curriculum knowledge that is required to ensure students have a robust understanding of each content point. In this case students must first know and understand the animal cell and the plant cell before they can identify the similarities and differences.

One way to determine the curriculum knowledge that should be selected from the broader content is to consider the concept of powerful knowledge. Powerful knowledge is described by Michael Young as referring to 'what the knowledge can do or what intellectual power it gives to those who have access to it' (Young, 2008). He develops this further: 'Powerful knowledge provides more reliable explanations and new ways of thinking about the world and acquiring it and can provide learners with a language for engaging in political, moral, and other kinds of debates' (2008).

Young developed this further to state knowledge is powerful 'if it predicts, if it explains, if it enables you to envisage alternatives' (Young, 2014). He defines knowledge as powerful if:

- It is distinct from the 'common sense' knowledge we acquire through our everyday experience.
- It is systematic.
- It is specialized.

Ultimately, powerful knowledge goes beyond our life experiences and serves to create integrated, inclusive, and shared learning. Subject curriculum should enrich the network of knowledge and the powerful knowledge we select should enable our students to participate in wider discussions, debate, and social and cultural opportunities.

Activity 1:
As a team take a point of content from the National Curriculum and identify the curriculum knowledge. Once you have identified the curriculum knowledge determine if this is powerful knowledge and why. A useful tool here is a knowledge organizer.

Threshold concepts
In 2003 Meyer and Land introduced the idea of threshold concepts.

'A threshold concept can be considered as akin to a portal, opening up a new and previously inaccessible way of thinking about something. It represents a transformed way of understanding, or interpreting, or viewing something without which the learner cannot progress' (Meyer and Land, 2003)

Put simply, a threshold concept helps students to develop the key concepts and skills that they need to progress. For example, in mathematics fractions would be considered a threshold concept. Fractions are introduced in the foundation stage of learning and are used throughout mathematics and across all areas within the subject and across other subject disciplines. Threshold concepts span different topics and help students to assimilate new information and develop and extend schema. New knowledge can be linked to a threshold concept and can change how students think.

When designing the curriculum, it is important to consider the threshold concepts in each subject and whether you do this implicitly (integrated into your existing curriculum model) or explicitly (a curriculum model based on threshold concepts) will be for you to determine. Cousin (2006) discusses the importance of considering threshold concepts on curriculum design and refers to them as 'jewels in the curriculum'.

Without students having a strong conceptual understanding of the threshold concept they may be unable to progress any further both in that specific area or satellite areas (both within the subject and across other subject disciplines). For example, if a student does not have strong conceptual understanding of equivalent fractions, then their understanding of fractional arithmetic is fragile. There is no single definitive list of threshold concepts, however, Meyer and Land (2003) identified five key characteristics: transformative, probably irreversible, integrative, bounded, potentially troublesome. Transformation sees a change in perception or understanding of the area studied and that change in perspective is likely to be retained in long-term memory. Integrative and bounded link to the awakening of connections and new conceptual areas which are sometimes specific to a particular discipline. Troublesome refers to the fact that threshold concepts can be challenging for students to grasp.

As teachers we are considered subject 'experts' and there is an assumption we have already mastered the threshold concepts and see the knowledge as implicit. Our role is to identify each concept within our curriculum to ensure we can develop the novice learner towards mastery. There is a danger because of our 'expert' status we can assume an understanding or prior experience thus making it more challenging to identify the transformative and irreversible knowledge. A starting point is to reflect on common barriers that students may encounter or

Introducing the curriculum

have previously encountered and to pinpoint whether this is linked to an underlying concept or simply poor implementation. Identification is of course only the first stage of the process because next we must consider how we will ensure we develop each threshold concept and of course what happens if students do not develop their conceptual understanding.

For a student to master a threshold this takes time and is a consequence of the careful construction of knowledge. Meyer and Land (2005) discuss the students being in a 'liminal state' before they reach this point, for example, in mathematics a student may be able to identify an equivalent fraction and can therefore complete this 'process' but they do not understand the 'why'. This 'liminal state' is being able to do the 'what' without the conceptual understanding. The role of memory and cognitive science is intertwined with curriculum development that is based implicitly or explicitly on threshold concepts. How we ensure we effectively implement the threshold concepts is something which needs careful consideration and consistency. When a student changes teacher or moves group, they should have the same learning experience and the threshold concepts should be 'taught' in the same way to ensure that as we progress horizontally and vertically through the curriculum learners can develop their schema. The importance of knowledge selection and sequencing is discussed further in Chapter 2.

The composite and component model

The composite and component model is becoming one of the more common curriculum models. A composite is the over-arching learning outcome(s) for the curriculum 'unit' knowledge. It provides the higher-level overview. The composite is then broken down into 'chunks' known as components as illustrated in Figure 1.3. A component may be a single lesson, or it may be more than one lesson. Our values and curriculum principles run throughout the curriculum from intent through to each component and we explore this model in depth in Chapters 2 and 3.

Summary

Sequencing of the curriculum is much more than the ordering of its component parts. It is about the relationships and connections between them, and the deeper understanding that the sequence allows our students to develop, strengthening schema and making long-term memory. As we progress through this book the theme of knowledge, specifically powerful curriculum knowledge, remains at

Introducing the curriculum

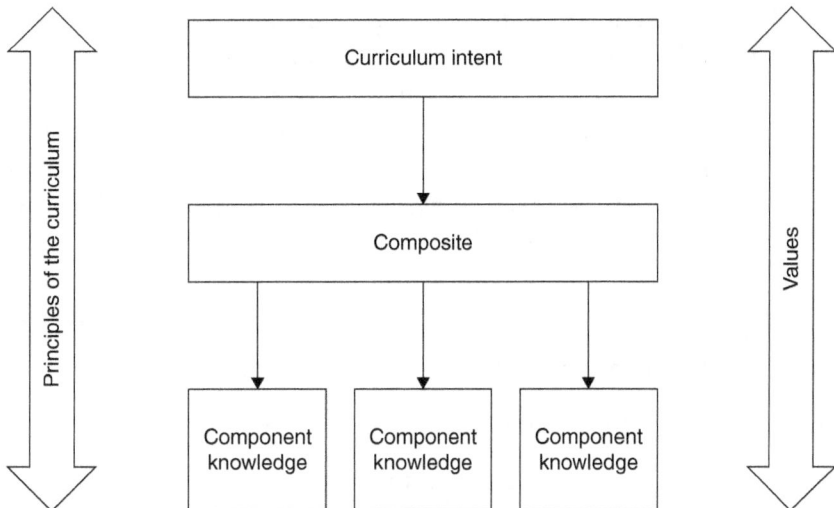

Figure 1.3 The composite and component structure

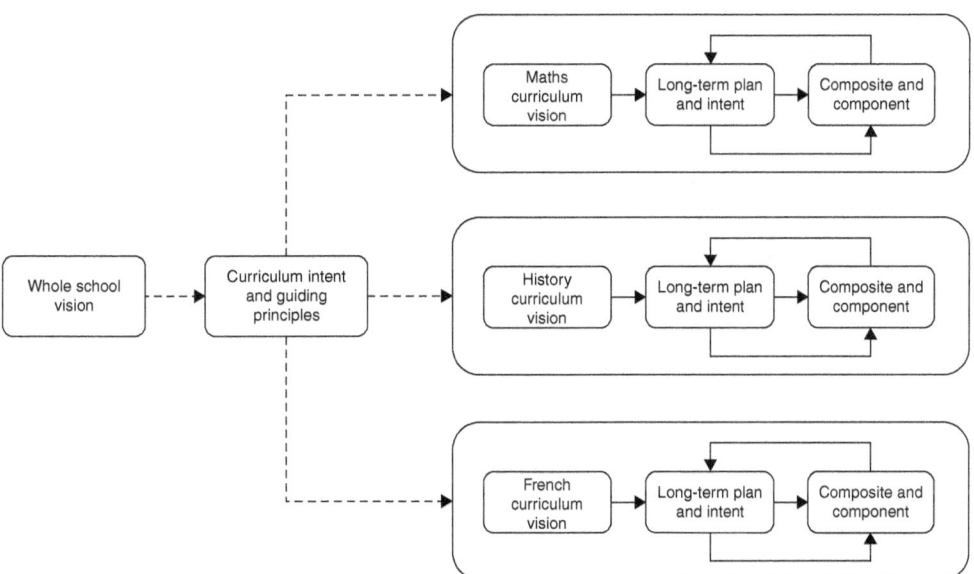

Figure 1.4 An illustration of whole school vision to subject-specific components. The arrows show a cycle of review (note only three subjects are shown as an example)

the heart of development. Time should be spent in depth with teams at all levels focusing on the 'what' and the 'how' we want students to learn.

The first step in our curriculum design is the whole school vision and translating this to curriculum intent. From this, subjects will develop their vision and intent statements which in turn support the identification of composite knowledge and component knowledge. This translates the curriculum from intent to implementation and is summarized in Figure 1.4.

Checklist:

- Have you defined your school vision and mission statement?
- Are your school values explicit?
- What are the pillars of your curriculum?
- Does your curriculum intent embrace the vision, values, and core principles?
- Have you identified the threshold concepts and are these implicit or explicit in your curriculum model?
- How do your subject curriculum interconnect?
- How consistent is the curriculum development across your teams?

Chapter 2

Understanding and developing the composite and component model

In Chapter 1 we introduced the curriculum hierarchy. In this chapter we develop the curriculum intent and explore further the composite and component model. Curriculum development within a subject begins with the long-term plan and in this chapter we consider the initial phases of curriculum development.

The long-term plan

The long-term subject plan is a higher-level document which includes the subject intent statement. It maps what students will learn and typically covers the content that is taught over the duration of the course. An example template is shown in Figure 2.1.

Subject Long-Term Plan

Subject Intent Statement

High Level Plan

	Term 1	Term 2	Term 3
Year a			
Year b			
Year c			

Figure 2.1 An example of a long-term plan template

Understanding and developing the composite and component model

A subject-level intent statement sets out 'what' you want the students to learn at each stage of the curriculum, 'why', and in 'what order'. The key features of a high-quality subject intent statement include:

1. An understanding of the purpose of study, the 'why'.

2. A clear rationale for the content knowledge that is included and how that content knowledge is sequenced.

3. How the knowledge will be assessed.

Examples of extracts from intent statements are shown in Figures 2.2 and 2.3.

Key Stage 1 (KS1; ages 5 to 7) History Intent Statement

The key stage 1 history curriculum aims to ignite students' passion for exploring the past through key historic events and characters. The curriculum has been sequenced in reverse chronological order to support students with understanding the concept of time and change. With each step back in time students will compare and contrast life in Britain, through the themes of lifestyle, transportation, innovation and health care.

In year 1 students begin to develop an awareness of the past through comparing the childhood of their parents and grandparents to their own. They will make tangible comparisons: comparing toys and childhood artefacts, childhood games, modes of transport and travel, fashion and home design, noting similarities and differences. Students will use different sources both primary and secondary to develop their descriptive writing skills of "life in modern Britain".

Students will utilise the skills they have developed to explore Victorian Britain (1837 – 1901) and will look at the concept of continuity and change and will make connections, draw contrasts and look at trends. Students will understand the significant changes that occurred during this period including the invention of the telephone by Alexander Graham Bell (1876), the invention of the penny-farthing (1871), the invention of the car by Carl Benz (1886) and will be able to synthesis questions to form contrasting arguments and interpretations of the past. Students will explore how these changes combined with rapid growth of our cities led to changes in for example lifestyles, living standards, developments in technology, health and wellbeing.

Figure 2.2 An extract from a key stage 1 (KS1; ages 5 to 7) history intent statement

Understanding and developing the composite and component model

> *Key Stage 3 (KS3; ages 11 to 14) Mathematics Intent Statement*
>
> Mathematics is a universal language used creatively to model the world around us and predict how it might change and advance. Mathematics has rich connections across all subject disciplines and is used extensively in science, engineering, computing, geography and product design. Through the key stage 3 curriculum students will explore the interconnectivity of mathematics and the progressive development of mathematical concepts. This spiral curriculum creates opportunities to integrate new knowledge through application, exposing students to a wide variety of problems and develop their skills to reason mathematically with increasing sophistication. Students become fluent in mathematics by developing conceptual understanding of the key underlying mathematical processes and their ability to interchange between different mathematical representations. All mathematical processes and methodology are carefully selected and sequenced to ensure students are able to identify connections within the subject discipline in both a direct and applied context.
>
> In year 7 students will know how to:
>
> - simplify algebraic expressions by collecting like terms and applying the concepts developed in 'number'
> - multiply a single term over a bracket
> - substitute values in algebraic formulae and expressions including positive and negative integers
> - substitute into scientific formulae and write sentence answers to problems demonstrating their ability to reason mathematically
>
> Knowledge will be assessed through routine direct questions which evaluate the student's ability to use implicit algebraic skills and students will be assessed on their ability to apply their knowledge in algebra to a problem in a different context.

Figure 2.3 An extract from a key stage 3 (KS3; ages 11 to 14) mathematics intent statement

If the subject is taught across multiple phases within the same school setting, then the long-term plan would map this period. For example, where mathematics is taught from key stage 3 to key stage 5, the long-term plan would map the

Understanding and developing the composite and component model

knowledge progressively across all key stages from year 7 to year 13 and development should be evident.

Composite and component structure

In Chapter 1 we introduced the composite and component structure where the composite knowledge is the over-arching learning outcome(s) which is formed through careful consideration of the component knowledge.
In developing the composite:

- be specific; for example, if we are studying the cellular biology simply stating 'cells' is not specific whereas to know the 'structure of animal and plant cells' would be specific content knowledge.

- be concise; it is not necessary to include all component knowledge as this level of detail would be provided in the medium-term plan.

- identify additional knowledge being taught where composites are revisited, for example if we study solving equations in year 7 and we revisit this in year 8 then it is important we have highlighted how year 8 builds on the knowledge from year 7.

If we consider an example of a composite from key stage 3 (KS3; ages 11 to 14) biology: 'to understand how plants produce glucose through photosynthesis and to know what affects the rate of photosynthesis'.

We can break this composite down into smaller pieces of knowledge called components.

- Students will know that photosynthesis is a chemical reaction that takes place in the leaves of a plant.

- Students will know that chlorophyll which is found in the cells converts carbon dioxide and water using light to produce oxygen and glucose.

- Students will know the word equation for photosynthesis.

- Students will know the chemical equation for photosynthesis.

- Students will know what affects the rate of photosynthesis (for example, temperature, light intensity, concentration of carbon dioxide and the amount of chlorophyll).

Understanding and developing the composite and component model

It is important to note that this is the key knowledge we expect our students to learn at that particular point in their curriculum journey, and it is not an exhaustive list. In this composite, for example, we are not looking at how the plant stores glucose and therefore we do not include that specific knowledge point. It is likely to be covered later in the curriculum and would be identified as a revisited and reactivated topic. In Chapter 3 we will explore further how we develop the composite into its component parts.

The high-level plan

Once the subject intent is established, the next phase of curriculum development is to develop the high-level plan. This details the order we teach and revisit curriculum knowledge and is where we articulate how learning develops underpinned by our rationale for sequencing. Examples of extracts from high-level plans are shown in Figures 2.4 and 2.5.

Key Stage 1 History High Level Plan

Year	1	
Term	1	2
Time Period	Recent History How does life today compare to life in the 1960's?	Victorian Britain 1807 - 1901 How does life in Victorian Britain compare to life in modern Britain?
Curriculum knowledge	• Comparing life in 1960's to life in modern Britain today. • Understanding how modes of transports have changed. • Know that health care is provided by the NHS and this is freely accessible to all. • Understand and explore how fashion has changed. • Know how technology has influenced changes in lifestyle. • Know and compare a typical school day.	• Identify and compare life in the 1960's to life in Victorian Britain. • Understand the different modes of transport. • Know that Victorian Britain was a period of change and development with significant inventions. • Compare the modern health system with Victorian Britain. • Explore living standards, sanitation and the impact on disease. • Contrast different fashions and access to textiles. • Understand different roles in society, jobs and the rich and the poor.
Curriculum concepts	Similarity and difference Continuity and change	Similarity and difference Continuity and change
Curriculum themes	Lifestyle Technology development Health and wellbeing Transportation Education	Social development Cultural development Technology development Health and wellbeing Lifestyles

Figure 2.4 An extract from a KS1 history high-level plan

Understanding and developing the composite and component model

Key Stage 3 Mathematics High-Level Plan

Term	1	
Topic	The language of algebra	Solving equations and inequalities
Year 7	• Students will know how to simplify algebraic expressions by collecting like terms. • Students will know how to multiply a single term over a bracket. • Students will know how to form algebraic expressions in an applied context. • Students will know how to substitute values into algebraic formulae and expressions. • Students will be able to substitute into scientific formulae and write sentence answers to problems.	• Students will be able to solve linear multi-step equations where the variable appears on one side (including where problems involve expanding a single term over a single bracket). • Students know how to form and solve equations in the context of simple geometry, for example, perimeter, area and angle geometry.
Year 8	• Students will know how to apply the laws of indices to simplify algebraic expressions. • Students will know how to factorise an expression by taking out common factors. • Students will know how to expand products of two binomials. • Students will know how to change the subject of the formulae by rearranging.	• Students will be able to solve linear multi-step equations where the variable appears on both sides of the equals (including where problems involve expanding a term over single bracket or where cross multiplication is needed). • Students know how to form and solve equations in the context of geometrical application, for example, properties 2D shapes, mathematical comprehension and manipulation of algebraic expressions.

Figure 2.5 An extract a KS3 mathematics high-level plan

The high-level plan provides a visual of how composite knowledge is sequenced and organized within the curriculum. It is a concise summary of 'what' students are going to learn. It may include an overview of themes running parallel to the development of specific content knowledge and how common threads develop and grow through the curriculum. The explicit detail of the knowledge taught in each component, however, is not addressed in the long-term plan but in the medium-term plan and we discuss this in greater depth in Chapter 3. Note that curriculum development is a cycle of improvement, and no doubt within your curriculum teams you will draft, redraft, and revisit your curriculum documentation many times.

Considerable time should be dedicated to the concept of curriculum sequencing. A well-sequenced curriculum which has a strategy to integrate prior knowledge has an effect size of +0.93 (Hattie, 2009). This means that a well-sequenced curriculum can considerably advance a student's achievement. However, we should take a moment to pause and reflect; in reality, there is no one-size-fits-all approach and there is no such thing as the perfectly sequenced curriculum. Instead, there is a continual drive to improve, where we strive to ensure our curriculum is developed to maximize learning through on-going curriculum dialogue.

Bjork and Bjork (2011) state 'learning requires an active process of interpretation— that is, mapping new things we are trying to learn onto what we already know'. Bruner (1966) also discusses the impact sequencing and revisiting has on the student's ability to master the curriculum knowledge. He states: 'Instruction consists of leading the learner through a sequence of statements and restatements of a problem or body of knowledge that increase the learner's ability to grasp, transform, and transfer what he is learning' (1966, p. 49). The high-level plan provides a visual of learning: new and revisited knowledge.

When sequencing the curriculum consideration needs to be given to structure of the knowledge, this has implications on 'how' this knowledge is developed throughout the curriculum. Within each subject area the interconnectivity of knowledge is different. In subjects such as mathematics, languages, and science the knowledge structure is hierarchical, meaning that there is an element of order to the curriculum knowledge. For example, in mathematics in order to solve simultaneous equations you must have a secure knowledge in substitution, rearranging formula and be able to solve linear equations in one variable. Whereas in subjects such as humanities and drama the knowledge structure has a more cumulative framework, meaning that knowledge is built upon and integrates with previous knowledge.

A high-level plan should include:

1. How the composite knowledge is sequenced through the curriculum.

2. Progression mapped horizontally and vertically through key themes or threshold concepts.

3. The composite knowledge for each 'block' of learning is clear.

4. The allocated amount of curriculum time needed to teach each composite.

There needs to be coherence between the subject intent and the high-level plan. The curriculum knowledge choices and the order they occur in your curriculum must match the intent statement. Figure 2.6 is an extract from a long-term plan for KS1 history.

In Figure 2.6 the curriculum knowledge has been sequenced in reverse chronological order as described in the subject intent statement. The developing themes of living standards, transport, innovation, and health care are integrated across the curriculum. The modern history of Britain is explicit in the curriculum documentation.

The amount of time dedicated to each composite will be determined by past learning experiences as much as the new curriculum mapping process. The reality is that time is at a premium, we cannot delve into the depths of each area of our subject, which is why the identification of specific content knowledge is critical and sufficient time should be spent discussing in curriculum teams and with senior leaders to ensure you are identifying the right and best content for each composite and the curriculum as a whole. Indeed, the long-term plan should be revisited regularly once the medium-term planning phase of curriculum development has begun, a 'temperature check'. Often the sequencing needs tweaking to support students' progression through the curriculum and this is where the 'lived' experience of curriculum delivery and review comes into play.

Role of memory and revisiting the curriculum

Our working memory has limited capacity, and a well-sequenced curriculum will reduce cognitive load by drawing upon and revisiting previous knowledge. Hermann Ebbinghaus (1885) forgetting curve research has implications on learning. Figure 2.7 illustrates the effect the time elapsed since first learning the content has on the percentage of knowledge retained.

The effects of the curve support us in building opportunities into our curriculum for students to revisit and retrieve knowledge and to be able to apply it in different contexts. Figure 2.8 shows the effect of the recall and retrieval on retention.

Understanding and developing the composite and component model

Key Stage 1 (KS1; ages 5 to 7) History Intent Statement

The key stage 1 history curriculum aims to ignite students' passion for exploring the past through key historic events and characters. The curriculum has been sequenced in reverse chronological order to support students with understanding the concept of time and change. With each step back in time students will compare and contrast life in Britain, through the themes of lifestyle, transportation, innovation and health care.

In year 1 students begin to develop an awareness of the past through comparing the childhood of their parents and grandparents to their own. They will make tangible comparisons: comparing toys and childhood artefacts, childhood games, modes of transport and travel, fashion and home design, noting similarities and differences. Students will use different sources both primary and secondary to develop their descriptive writing skills of "life in modern Britain".

Students will utilise the skills they have developed to explore Victorian Britain (1837–1901) and will look at the concepts of continuity and change and will make connections, draw contrasts and look at trends. Students will understand the significant changes that occurred during this period including the invention of the telephone by Alexander Graham Bell (1876), the invention of the penny-farthing (1871), the invention of the car by Carl Benz (1886) and will be able to synthesis questions to form contrasting arguments and interpretations of the past. Students will explore how these changes combined with rapid growth of our cities led to changes in for example lifestyles, living standards, developments in technology, health and wellbeing.

Key Stage 1 History High Level Plan

Year	1		
Term	1		2
Time period	Recent History		Victorian Britain 1807–1901
	How does life today compare to life in the 1960's?		How does life in Victorian Britain compare to life in modern Britain?
Curriculum knowledge	• Comparing life in 1960's to life in modern Britain today. • Understanding how modes of transports have changed. • Know that health care is provided by the NHS and this is freely accessible to all. • Understand and explore how fashion has changed. • Know how technology has influenced changes in lifestyle. • Know and compare a typical school day.		• Identify and compare life in the 1960's to life in Victorian Britain. • Understand the different modes of transport. • Know that Victorian Britain was a period of change and development with significant inventions. • Compare the modern health system with Victorian Britain. • Explore living standards, sanitation and the impact on disease. • Contrast different fashions and access to textiles. • Understand different roles in society, jobs and the rich and the poor.
Curriculum concepts	Similarity and difference Continuity and change		Similarity and difference Continuity and change
Curriculum themes	Lifestyle Technology development Health and wellbeing Transportation Education		Social development Cultural development Technology development Health and wellbeing Lifestyles

Figure 2.6 An example from KS1 history to illustrate the coherence between the subject intent statement and the high-level plan

23

Understanding and developing the composite and component model

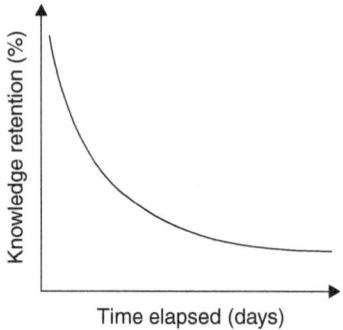

Figure 2.7 An example of an illustration of the Hermann Ebbinghaus (1885) forgetting curve

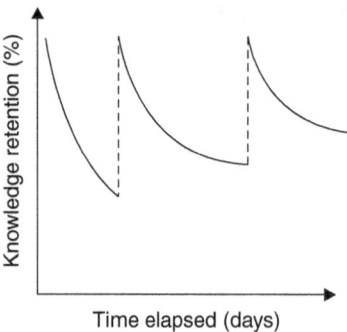

Figure 2.8 An example of an illustration of how revisiting the knowledge can impact on retention

By revisiting the curriculum knowledge, we require students to recall information and therefore strengthen schema. Revisiting knowledge throughout the curriculum is important in supporting the student to store the information into the long-term memory. In Chapter 4 the role of knowledge recall and memory is discussed when designing a lesson. Each time we revisit the curriculum knowledge the time lag between the next revisit can be lengthened and increases the likelihood of remembering.

When ordering the curriculum, plan explicitly for how content will be revisited as the curriculum progresses (note this is with reference to the development of a 'topic' and not revisiting based on the revisiting of content identified through assessment where students did not retain the knowledge – this cannot be foreseen). Making links to prior knowledge is important to strengthen and develop schema. There are different curriculum organizational tools when sequencing the curriculum and many ways that the curriculum can be organized, including spaced, interleaved, and spiral. There is not a perfect approach to curriculum design and the structure of your curriculum will be dependent on your subject area and context.

In a spaced curriculum students are provided with opportunities to revisit and practise the content. The concept of the spaced curriculum evolved from the research by Hermann Ebbinghaus which followed the development of the forgetting curve. An interleaved curriculum involves teaching different concepts or skills at alternating points rather than teaching each concept or skill in a discrete and separate unit. The high-level plan maps out how the switching between composites takes place and which episodes of learning are taught and there is a common thread. There is no prescriptive formula for which content or subjects should be interleaved. This is guided by the principles of your curriculum. In a curriculum that is not interleaved the learning episodes are taught one at a time in succession.

A spiral curriculum is similar, but not the same as, a spaced and interleaved curriculum. The content is studied throughout the curriculum and with each iteration the subject matter increases in depth. Within a spiral curriculum it is important to identify prior knowledge (but remember not to assume this) to ensure that assessment can be used effectively as a diagnostic tool.

In a spaced, interleaved and spiral curriculum model new learning is embedded in the long-term memory through repetition and active recall.

Quality assuring the long-term plan

It is important throughout the curriculum development process that all documents are regularly reviewed, and this should include professional dialogue and challenge. In this chapter we focus on quality assurance of curriculum documents and in Chapter 7 we will discuss quality assurance of the implementation of the curriculum.

Quality assuring a curriculum you have not yet implemented is a natural challenge. The first stage should therefore be to question leaders thinking about their curriculum design. Specific questions about the curriculum can be useful in this process:

- What are the important concepts within your curriculum? Show me an example of how this is developed.

Understanding and developing the composite and component model

- Can you give me an example of how the curriculum pillar 'X' features in your curriculum?
- Why have you chosen to teach solving equations before finding the area of a compound shape?
- In the high-level plan students are taught photosynthesis twice. Why have you chosen to revisit this in the curriculum? What is the difference between the two composites?
- How is the students' knowledge in key stage 2 built upon in key stage 3? Give me an example of this.
- How have you chosen the end points of your curriculum?

For these curriculum conversations to be meaningful you do not need to be a subject expert, however, you do need to have a reasonable understanding of the subject matter itself. The reviewer should use the prompts below as a check in:

- Have you read the long-term plan before the meeting and checked the coherence between the subject intent and high-level plan? Is the curriculum knowledge and sequencing the same in the intent statement and high-level plan?
- Have you read the national curriculum for the subject you are reviewing? It is a worthwhile task to highlight which knowledge from the national curriculum is evident in the long-term plan. This will enable to you to have a discussion with the subject leader if there are discrepancies between the national curriculum and long-term plan.
- Are the pillars of the curriculum evident?
- What are the threshold concepts/powerful knowledge?

Peer review is also an important part of the quality assurance process and allows the learning conversations to develop at all levels within your school.

Summary

The resounding theme is sequencing at all levels of curriculum development. Developing an effective long-term plan requires careful consideration of the order in which you present new knowledge and the rationale for doing so.

Understanding and developing the composite and component model

The curriculum should be a progression model where new knowledge builds on existing knowledge, with opportunities to revisit and reactivate. This may utilize the interleaved, spaced or spiral curriculum model.

Checklist

Intent statement

- Does the subject vision align with the whole school vision?
- Is the rationale for sequencing the curriculum clear?
- Does the sequencing of the curriculum provide optimum conditions for students to activate prior knowledge to develop new knowledge?
- Are the content choices ambitious? They should be at least as challenging as the national curriculum.
- Are the 'powerful knowledge' or threshold concepts of your curriculum clearly articulated?

High-level plan

- Is there a clear link between the intent statement and the high-level plan?
- Is the content outlined in the intent statement evident in the high-level plan?
- Is the curriculum sequenced as outlined in the intent statement?
- Can you clearly identify the threshold concepts or powerful knowledge of the curriculum?
- Is there evidential progression?
- Is the rationale for assessment of the curriculum clear?
- Are the end points of the curriculum identified and do they take account of and develop from the end points of the previous curriculum phase? How do the end points enable transition to the next phase of learning?

Quality assuring the curriculum

- Is it clear 'what' knowledge the teacher wants students to learn?
- Is the knowledge selected ambitious?

Understanding and developing the composite and component model

- Is the sequencing of the curriculum clear?
- What is the rationale for sequencing?
- Is sequencing consistent in the medium-term plan and does sequencing support the development of knowledge into the long-term memory?
- How does the knowledge develop?

Chapter 3

Identifying curriculum knowledge

In the long-term plan we identified the composite knowledge and each composite forms a medium-term plan. In the medium-term plan the composite knowledge is broken down into component knowledge. The medium-term plan is then used by teachers to create learning episodes which bring the curriculum to life. An episode is not necessarily a lesson. A single lesson may have several learning episodes or a single learning episode may happen over one or more lessons. An example template is shown in Figure 3.1.

Unit Title - Year X Medium Term Plan

Composite:	Term:	Number of Hours:
Key knowledge and how it will be developed:	Knowledge for scaffolding:	Deepening the knowledge:
Component 1		
Component 2		
Component 3		
Component 4		
Component 5		

Interim and End of Composite Assessment	Disciplinary Literacy
Homework	Cultural Capital

Figure 3.1 An example of a medium-term plan template

Identifying curriculum knowledge

The medium-term plan is a subject-specific document and should outline:

- How composite knowledge is broken down into component knowledge.
- How component knowledge is sequenced.
- How to scaffold the curriculum to ensure all students will acquire the component knowledge.
- How students can deepen their understanding of the component knowledge.
- How the composite and component knowledge is going to be assessed.
- How the curriculum pillars are visited in the composite. For example, if numeracy is a pillar of the curriculum, then opportunities to teach numeracy in context should be identified.

Breaking down the composite knowledge

We discussed the importance of investing time within curriculum teams to think about how we break down composite knowledge into component knowledge. This process should:

- Provide clarity for teachers as to the specific content knowledge and vocabulary to teach, the methods to use (these should be consistent across teachers and horizontally and vertically throughout the curriculum to ensure that optimum development of learning and memory) and how learning can be supported by avoiding cognitive overload.
- Enable effective sequencing of knowledge. By specifying what you want students to learn you can effectively sequence and determine prior knowledge.

Breaking down the composite knowledge into its component knowledge requires you to have an appreciation of different categories of knowledge within your subject area. Curriculum knowledge takes many forms, the main categories of knowledge are:

- Substantive
- Disciplinary
- Declarative

- Procedural
- Hinterland

Substantive knowledge is the body of knowledge that we teach as fact, such as, rules and concepts. It involves concepts which form the underpinning structure of the subject. Examples of substantive knowledge are:

- Pythagoras' theorem in mathematics.
- Mitosis in science.

Disciplinary knowledge is the process that an expert in the subject field uses to establish, validate, and/or review the substantive knowledge. The amount of disciplinary knowledge within each subject area will vary and is dependent on the ages of the students that you teach (Counsell, 2018a). For example, in mathematics students aged 6 will not be able to work effectively with algebraic proof as they have not developed the substantive knowledge required.

Examples of disciplinary knowledge are:

- Testing hypotheses in science.
- Assessing the reliability of a source in history.
- Analysing choropleth maps detailing the amount of rainfall in geography.

An efficient and effective curriculum should carefully consider the sequencing of both substantive and disciplinary knowledge and the role they have in developing students' curriculum knowledge by working together (Ofsted, 2021). How the two types of knowledge are intertwined and develop together should be evident in the medium-term plan, as illustrated in Figure 3.2.

Declarative knowledge is the facts, theories, and concepts that are true. Declarative knowledge is conscious and focuses on the 'what' rather than the 'why' or the 'how'. Examples of declarative knowledge are:

- The boiling point of water is 100°C.
- The earth consists of the crust, the mantle, the outer core and the inner core.
- Linguistic structure or form.

Procedural knowledge is the knowledge of how to do something. Examples of procedural knowledge are:

Identifying curriculum knowledge

Substantive knowledge (Extract)	Disciplinary knowledge
Students will know that the Nazis used public rallies to spread propaganda, such as the 1936 Berlin Olympics to show off German wealth and power. Students will know that propaganda was used to change culture and society, for example, modern art was banned in favour of paintings aligned with Nazi ideology and school textbooks were rewritten to make Germans look successful.	Students will think historically and be able to analyse sources demonstrating Nazi propaganda techniques. They will consider: • The type of source. • The date the source was created. • The meaning and interpretation of the source. • The person who created the source and their viewpoint. • The historical context at the time the source was created. • The purpose of the source. Students will be able to compare different sources.

Figure 3.2 An example of a component from a history medium-term plan which develops both substantive and disciplinary knowledge

- How to balance a chemical equation.
- How to use the bridge method to cut vegetables.
- How to add two fractions, where each fraction is less than 1, with different denominators.

Figure 3.3 shows how procedural knowledge can be illustrated in the medium-term plan.

To develop conceptual understanding a deliberate choice needs to be made on the method students should use. This method should be explicitly modelled in the medium term to ensure a consistent approach across teachers. Remember the greatest variability is often within rather than between schools and detailed medium-term plans will limit the impact of the individual teacher on content or process knowledge. If the explicit model is not included in the medium-term plan, then naturally teachers will select what they determine to be the 'best method' and imagine the impact if a 'topic' is studied in year 7, revisited in year 8 and again in year 9, the student has a different teacher in year 7, 8, and 9 and learns 'three different methods'. The outcome is confusion at best. Compare this to a student having different teachers in year 7, 8, and 9, the topic being re-visited each year but the 'method' being the same. The outcome, learning is developed progressively, potentially leading to mastery.

Identifying curriculum knowledge

Component

Students will know how to add two fractions, where each fraction is less than 1, with different denominators.

Developing the method

$$\frac{2}{5} + \frac{1}{3}$$

Fractions can only be added if the denominators are the same. To find a **common denominator**, list the **multiples** of the denominators for both fractions and identify the **lowest common multiple**. If the lowest common multiple is used then you will not need to simplify at the end.

Multiples of 5 are: 5, 10, 15, 20
Multiples of 3 are: 3, 6, 9, 12, 15

The lowest common multiple of 5 and 3 is 15.

Write each fraction as an **equivalent fraction** using the denominator found above.

$$\frac{2}{5} = \frac{6}{15}$$

$$\frac{1}{3} = \frac{5}{15}$$

Add the two **numerators** together. The **denominator** remains the same.

$$\frac{6}{15} + \frac{5}{15}$$

$$= \frac{6+5}{15}$$

$$= \frac{11}{15}$$

Simplify the fraction, if required.

Figure 3.3 An example from key stage 2 mathematics where procedural knowledge of adding fractions is developed

Identifying curriculum knowledge

It is important to limit the number of different methods (conceptual or process driven) within the curriculum; this is to avoid cognitive overload and free up space in the working memory. Fewer methods that can be applied to multiple contexts within not only your subject area but cross-curricular, will support the development of students' long-term memory.

The concept of knowledge being categorized as core or hinterland was first outlined by Christine Counsell (2018b); core knowledge is residual knowledge that you want the students to 'remember' and hinterland is the contextual knowledge that 'makes curriculum work as narrative' (2018b).

Examples of hinterland knowledge are:

- The story of the apple falling on the head of Isaac Newton when teaching gravity in science.

- Listening to the personal experiences of people who lived through the Second World War when learning about the impact of the war in history.

Careful selection of hinterland knowledge is needed to ensure it is not a distraction to the learning of the core knowledge.

Deconstructing the composite knowledge

The first step in developing a medium-term plan is to identify the composite end points. For example, in history it is impossible to teach all the events that led up to the Second World War. Without identifying the end points, the composite knowledge will not be able to be deconstructed effectively into the component knowledge.

Once the end points are identified, a step-by-step approach should be taken to deconstruct the composite:

1. List **all** the component knowledge.

2. Identify which component knowledge would have been **encountered earlier** in the curriculum and when. This is the knowledge that will need to be 'reactivated'.

3. Be **specific** in the knowledge for each component including the content, vocabulary, and any choice of method.

4. Carefully consider how this will be **sequenced**.

Identifying curriculum knowledge

An example of deconstructing the composite knowledge for a key stage 3 computer science (KS3; ages 11 to 14) is shown below:

Example 1:
Composite: How do computers process data using binary?

Step 1: Listing the component knowledge:

- Students will know what a binary number is.
- Students will know how binary numbers can be used to represent text and images.
- Students will know what a denary number is.
- Students will know why numbers are written in binary.
- Students will know how to convert a denary number to a binary number.
- Students will know how to add and subtract numbers written in binary.
- Students will know what overflow is.
- Students will know why computers need to use binary data.
- Students will know what the powers of 2 are and how they relate to binary numbers.
- Students will know how to convert a binary number to a denary number.

Step 2: Identifying prior knowledge.
Students will be familiar with denary numbers through their work in mathematics, however, they are unlikely to know that the base system they are using in mathematics is denary.

Step 3: Sequence the components.
The order of the components is:

1. Students will know why computers need to use binary data.
2. Students will know what a denary number is.
3. Students will know what a binary number is.
4. Students will know what the powers of 2 are and how they relate to binary numbers.

Identifying curriculum knowledge

5. Students will know why numbers are written in binary.

6. Students will know how to convert a denary number to a binary number.

7. Students will know how to convert a binary number to a denary number.

8. Students will know how to add and subtract numbers written in binary.

Component: how computers use binary to represent images.

Students will know that for a computer to process images, the image needs to be converted to binary.

Students will know that a digital image is constructed using pixels. Each **pixel** is a building block of colour that is used to create an image. Each pixel is a binary number.

Students will know when an image is taken **metadata** is collected, this provides information about the image such as the size of the image.

Students will know how to represent a black and white image using binary.

1. Start with the black and white image. For every white pixel write 0 and for every black pixel write 1.

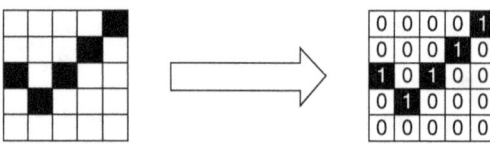

2. Starting at the top left of the image and working your way across and down write out the binary number.
   00001 00010 10100 01000 00000

Students will know that colour can be added to an image by increasing the number of bits per pixel.
- 1-bit per pixel: 2 colours
- 2-bit per pixel: 4 colours
- 3-bit per pixel: 8 colours

Figure 3.4 An example from key stage 3 computer science where the component knowledge is specified in detail

9. Students will know what overflow is.

10. Students will know how binary can be used to represent text.

11. Students will know how binary can be used to represent images.

Step 4: Specify the detail as shown in Figure 3.4 which provides an example of how the component knowledge may be specified.

Knowledge for scaffolding

The most important point to make here is that scaffolding is not a tool exclusively used to support low-ability learners; the working memory is limited and to avoid cognitive overload, scaffolding is used to elevate and support the formation of connections between prior knowledge and new knowledge. Once those connections are secure the scaffold is typically removed.

The medium-term plan outlines specific prior knowledge that requires 'activating' and should identify the scaffolding tools a teacher should use to support the development of new connections. Figure 3.5 is an example of how prior knowledge of animal cells is required to understand the adaptations of specialist cells.

Prior knowledge can broadly speaking be considered taught knowledge either explicitly through the subject curriculum or content or context covered in other subject curriculums or assumed knowledge (life experiences). Figure 3.6 is an example where the knowledge of Victorian Britain (History curriculum) provides context when teaching *Oliver Twist* (English Literature curriculum).

Of course, the knowledge of Victorian Britain would be needed to be taught before the teaching of *Oliver Twist* (by Charles Dickens) if this knowledge is to be activated. Herein lies the web of cross-curricular learning; in reality, rarely mastered.

When thinking about prior knowledge we must also consider 'assumed' knowledge. This is knowledge that comes from life experiences, such as, going on holiday or visiting an art gallery. A student whose 'life experience' allows them greater access to the curriculum is at an advantage. We discuss the impact of cultural and social capital on learning in Chapter 6. Figure 3.7 demonstrates how scaffolding can be used to support students who have knowledge gaps as a result of reduced cultural capital.

To support the learning of new material we may need to consider alternative methods; this might be particularly pertinent in subjects such as mathematics.

Identifying curriculum knowledge

Component	Knowledge for scaffolding
Students will know that the function of a sperm cell is to fertilise the egg cell. Students will know how a sperm cell has been adapted: 1. The genetic material is stored in the **nucleus** of the cell which is found in the head of the sperm cell. 2. The head of the sperm cell contains **enzymes** which digests the cell membrane of the egg upon penetration. 3. The middle of the sperm cell is packed with **mitochondria**. This is to provide energy so the sperm can swim. 4. Sperm cells have a **tail** which is used to swim towards the egg cell.	Students will need to be able to recall the structure of an animal cell and know the functions of each part of the cell: – cytoplasm – mitochondria – nucleus – cell membrane

Figure 3.5 An example from key stage 3 science demonstrating the activation of prior knowledge

---

Knowledge for scaffolding

Students will need to recall their knowledge from the history curriculum where they learned about life in Victorian Britain. Charles Dickens began publishing Oliver Twist in 1837 to 1839 at final publication, this was towards the start of the Victorian era.

In order to understand the context of the story in Oliver Twist students must have background knowledge of the living standards in Victorian Britain. This includes:
- The city of London was overcrowded.
- The age expectancy was low due to poor sanitation in London, many people died earlier than expected due to cholera.
- Victorian workhouses were designed to support people who had no money, they could live in the workhouse in exchange for completing work set by their guardians.
- The living conditions of the workhouses were cramped and unhygienic. Little food was given to those who lived there and it was often of poor quality.

Figure 3.6 An example from key stage 3 English literature showing explicit subject and contextual knowledge

Identifying curriculum knowledge

Component	Knowledge for scaffolding
Students will know how to write in the first-person narrative where they are setting the scene for the piece of creative writing. Students are expected to effectively describe the scene using the five senses in the first-person narrative. The students will be given a picture stimulus of a beach.	Students who have experienced a beach will have cultural capital advantage. Minimise impact by: • Watching a series video clips showing people on the beach. • Encourage whole class discussion to share experiences and thoughts. • Use the five senses to scaffold the student's thinking to imagine what they will see, hear, smell, taste and feel.

Figure 3.7 An example from key stage 4 English language of how scaffolding addresses reduced cultural capital

Any alternative method should not be 'one off' and should link to process or conceptual development that is used perhaps in other areas of the curriculum. The option of alternative methodology should be clearly identified. Figure 3.8 is an example from mathematics, where the grid method is suggested as a suitable alternative method to expanding double brackets. The grid method is a method used for multiplication introduced in the early phases of mathematical development for problems such as 32 x 48 and so we have not introduced a new method but have applied a previously taught method to a new problem involving algebra. This deepens learning. Scaffolding is discussed in greater depth in Chapter 4.

Opportunities to deepen understanding

In the medium-term plan opportunities for students to deepen their understanding of component knowledge should be identified. Opportunities to deepen understanding are not:

- More of the same, for example, in science you would not give the students more questions on finding the relative molecular mass of compound.
- 'Bigger' numbers, for example if you are studying adding whole numbers you would not give them larger numbers to add.
- Moving onto learning the next component in the sequence.

Identifying curriculum knowledge

Component	Knowledge for scaffolding
Students will know how to expand and simplify a pair of brackets. Developing the method Expand and simplify $(3x + 5)(2x - 3)$ Build on the concept of expanding a single bracket by multiplying everything in the first bracket by everything in the second bracket. $(3x + 5)(2x - 3)$ $6x^2 + 10x - 9x - 15$ Simplify by collecting the like terms. $6x^2 \;\widehat{+ 10x}\;\widehat{- 9x}\; - 15$ $= 6x^2 + x - 15$	Students can use the grid method as an alternative method to expand and simplify a pair of brackets. Expand and simplify $(3x + 5)(2x - 3)$ | × | $3x$ | $+ 5$ | |---|---|---| | $2x$ | $6x^2$ | $+ 10x$ | | -3 | $-9x$ | -15 | $6x^2 + 10x - 9x - 15$ Simplify by collecting the like terms. $6x^2 \;\widehat{+ 10x}\;\widehat{- 9x}\; - 15$ $= 6x^2 + x - 15$

Figure 3.8 An example from key stage 3 mathematics which illustrates knowledge of alternative methods

Using Bloom's taxonomy (1956) of cognition is a beneficial tool when designing opportunities for students to deepen their understanding, designing tasks where students are required to apply the newly acquired knowledge to a different context or to analyse and evaluate a different scenario using their knowledge.

The medium-term plan should identify where and what the opportunities are for students to deepen their understanding alongside what we expect the students to gain and how we expect their learning to develop. Examples of opportunities to deepen understanding are given in Figures 3.9 and 3.10.

Identifying curriculum knowledge

Component	Deepening the knowledge
Students will be able to describe a well-balanced diet using the five food groups: • Fruit and vegetables • Carbohydrates • Fibre • Protein • Fats and oils Students will know the health benefits of each of the food groups. Students will know the potential negative impacts of food groups. Students are able to compare and contrast food groups and make healthy choices.	Phillip has recently been diagnosed with heart disease. The doctors have told him to make changes to his diet. Recommend which foods Phillip should include and avoid in his diet. Justify your answer by giving reasons why.

Figure 3.9 An example of identifying opportunities to deepen understanding in food technology

Developing literacy across the curriculum

> Young people who leave school without good literacy skills are held back at every stage of life. Their outcomes are poorer on almost every measure, from health and wellbeing, to employment and finance.
>
> (EEF, 2021a)

Strong literacy teaching starts with vocabulary. There are three tiers of vocabulary as identified by Beck et al. (2002). These are:

- Tier 1 vocabulary are everyday words, for example, book and happy.
- Tier 2 vocabulary are words that appear across multiple subject areas, for example, evaluate and analyse.
- Tier 3 vocabulary are subject-specific words, for example, glaciation in geography and mitosis in science.

In each component tier 2 and 3 vocabularies should be identified. For tier 3 it is beneficial to have a definition of the word as well as details of the etymology

Identifying curriculum knowledge

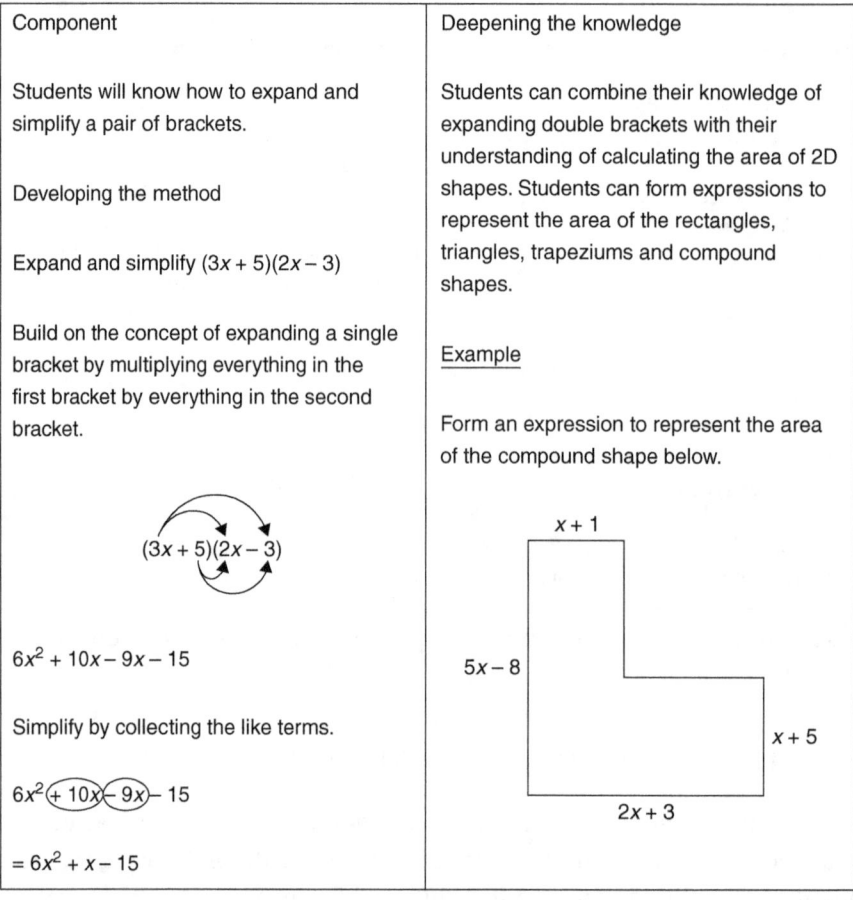

Figure 3.10 An example of identifying opportunities to deepen understanding in mathematics

(origin of the word) and morphology (structure of the word). This naturally supports the teaching of subject-specific vocabulary. An example is shown in Figure 3.11.

Disciplinary literacy is the literacy needed to effectively communicate within each subject area, as a subject expert orally and through written communication. Examples include how we write an evaluation in food technology or discuss a piece of music. We need to teach the students how to use tier 2 and 3 vocabulary coupled with subject-specific communication techniques. Figures 3.12 and 3.13 are examples of how the teaching of disciplinary literacy can be incorporated into the medium-term plan.

Identifying curriculum knowledge

> **Component**
>
> Students will know that a **hydrosphere** is the total amount of water that can be found on a planet.
>
> Etymology of hydrosphere
>
> The word hydrosphere can be split up into **hydro** which comes from the Greek root word for 'water' and **sphere** meaning 'globe'.

Figure 3.11 Identifying subject terminology within a geography component

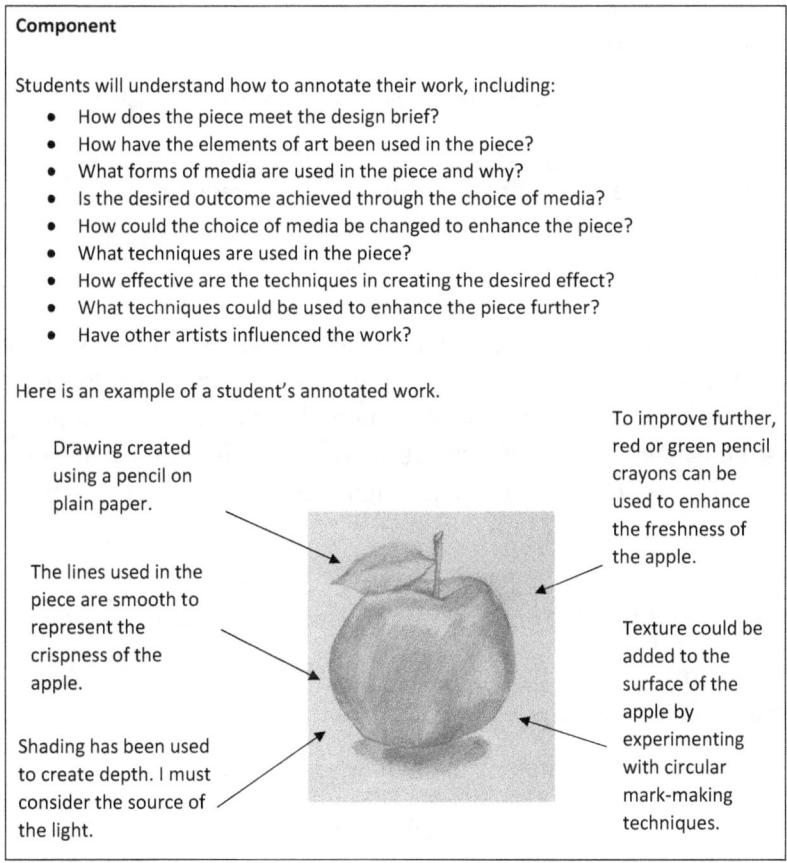

Figure 3.12 An example of developing disciplinary literacy in art

Identifying curriculum knowledge

Component

Students will know there are different elements of music. These include:

- dynamics
- tempo
- structure
- pitch
- duration
- texture

Students will know when evaluating a piece of music, they should describe:

- how the elements of music have been used
- how the element of music changes throughout the piece
- the intended effect on the listener

Students will apply their musical vocabulary to describe the elements of music, for example allegro for slow and piano for quiet

---

Figure 3.13 An example of developing disciplinary literacy in music

Summary

Specificity is the underlying theme when identifying curriculum knowledge. Be specific with every element of the medium-term plan from identifying the end points of the composite to the specific methodology and definitions you want students to know and use. Specificity within the medium-term plan means teachers should be clear as to 'what' needs to be taught and 'how' it should be taught.

Checklist

- Have you identified the end point for the composite knowledge?
- Have you broken down the composite knowledge into the component knowledge and ensured this is well sequenced?
- Have you ensured component knowledge is specific?
- Have you identified the knowledge needed for scaffolding?
- Have you identified the opportunities for students to deepen their knowledge?
- Have you identified the tier 2 and 3 vocabularies for each component?

Chapter 4

The learning cycle

There are countless articles and books written about or linked to the learning cycle. No doubt you have attended at least one professional development session focused on how to construct an outstanding lesson. Those who have been teaching for some time will have seen initiatives come and go in cycles from the focus on learning styles (remember visual, auditory, kinaesthetic VAK) to the three-part or five-part lesson. Each has their merit but is of little value if the focus is on construction.

Value in our lessons evolves through the development of learning underpinned by a fundamental understanding of cognitive load and the impact on working memory and long-term memory. We will explore in this chapter how we use recommendations from cognitive load theory to develop a lesson which develops progressive learning for all students.

A lesson can appear to engage students and yet have little to no impact when we assess the retention or application of knowledge (memory recall). This is where the quality of our quality assurance process is extremely important. In Chapter 7 we discuss how to create an effective quality assurance system. In this chapter we will re-visit and incorporate into our planning the following considerations from cognitive load theory (Cognitive load theory: Research that teachers really need to understand, September 2017, Centre for Education Statistics and Evaluation, Australia):

- There is a **limit** to how much **new information** the brain can process at any one time.

- There are **no known limits** to how much **stored information** can be processed at one time.

- Processing **new information** results in 'cognitive load' on **working memory** which can affect **learning outcomes.**

The learning cycle

Developing our lessons

The very best learning takes place when our curriculum allows students to progressively develop and retain their knowledge and skills. The vehicle through which we execute this is of course our lessons but no matter how 'good' our lessons appear on the surface if they are not bound by the core principles of memory then students will not learn or will not learn to their optimum level. A well-constructed curriculum is where we begin our journey starting with the long-term plan. Without this high-level planning learning can be disorganized and disjointed which leads to a learner who is not able to make connections, link concepts or progressively develop their knowledge. Figure 4.1 reminds us of the development of the curriculum from the long-term plan to the component.

'The reason experts remember more is that what novices see as separate pieces of information, experts see as organized sets of ideas' (Donovan & Bransford, 2005).

We need to begin by deconstructing our curriculum to ensure that it is well sequenced and supports lessons to embed and develop learning through key skills and knowledge. One of the things we notice most when we talk to those beginning their work on curriculum is that they focus on topics and lists of content rather than the progressive development of knowledge. Very often this can be the same sequence of topics as 20 years ago that have been completed year-in year-out with perhaps the only change being the format of the medium-term plan. When we talk to practitioners who are re-designing their curriculum they will often say 'but we are simply re-writing this in a different format or using a new template'. If you find yourself saying this then it is most probably true,

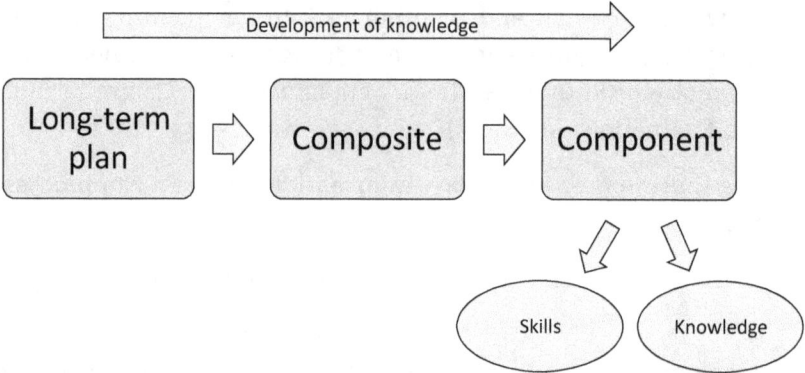

Figure 4.1 From the long-term plan to the component

The learning cycle

thus making the exercise pointless and we say this because when you make the shift from content to knowledge, focusing on developing memory, you will see a transformation in your curriculum mindset. Remember, to develop a world-class education system, we must challenge ourselves and our current thinking. Our starting point is to ask ourselves the following questions.
Through our curriculum:

1. Do we have a rich understanding of the powerful knowledge?
2. Do we understand the distinction between skills and knowledge?
3. What assumptions about prior knowledge have we made?
4. Have we considered the connections between pre-acquired and new knowledge?
5. Do we understand the basics of cognitive load theory and how this links to a learning cycle?
6. How are we going to interweave and sequence learning with a recognition of the cycle of past, present, and future knowledge (Figure 4.2) to achieve our curriculum goals?

In this chapter we will focus on a simple learning cycle and then look at how we develop a lesson and how we ensure that this builds on prior learning and embeds conceptual and process-driven knowledge. It is important to note at this point that while we talk about developing knowledge and memory this does not

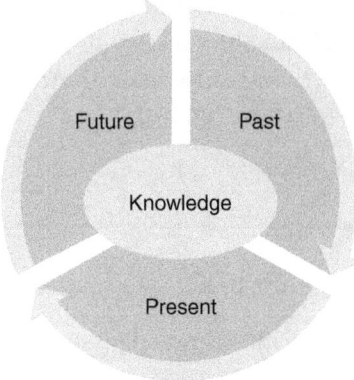

Figure 4.2 The cycle of knowledge. Our present knowledge becomes our future knowledge, and our future knowledge becomes our past knowledge

The learning cycle

mean simply creating a passive curriculum where students simply memorize a series of facts (rote-learning), but one where our students are actively involved in using their skills and conceptual foundations adding new knowledge and are able to apply this to different problem solving or independent thinking scenarios utilizing their working memory and embedding long-term memory.

Knowledge that is passively taught will have little to no impact. Indeed, the research conducted by Mehta and Fine (Meta & Fine, 2019) discusses that deeper learning emerges at the intersection of three virtues: *mastery*, *identity*, and *creativity*:

- Mastery: where students have opportunities to develop knowledge and skill.

- Identity: where they come to see their core selves as vitally connected to what they are learning and doing.

- Creativity: where they have opportunities to enact their learning by producing something rather than simply receiving knowledge.

We need to start thinking why we are planning our lessons and activities and how we think deeply about learning. The research by Hattie is summarized in the Visible Learning Plus (June, 2019). *250+ Influences on Student Achievement and in Hattie effect size list – 256 Influences Related To Achievement (visible-learning.org)*. Hattie researched the influence of different effects on student achievement. In 2015 he increased his meta-analyses from 800 to 1200. The meta-analysis of factors that influence student learning shows that the average effect size is 0.40 and Hattie referred to this as his 'hinge point'. It represented a year's growth per year of schooling for a student. Anything above +0.40 may therefore be an effect that accelerates student learning. Below are some of the positive impact strategies within the classroom that we need to keep in mind (*Hattie effect size list – 256 Influences Related To Achievement (visible-learning.org)* and Visible Learning Plus (June, 2019)).

- Collective teacher efficacy +1.57

- Cognitive task analysis +1.29

- Conceptual change programs +0.99

- Strategy to integrate with prior knowledge +0.93

- Classroom discussion +0.82

- Scaffolding +0.82

- Deliberate practice +0.79
- Summarization +0.79
- Planning and prediction +0.76
- Repeated reading programs +0.75
- Rehearsal and memorization +0.73
- Problem-solving teaching +0.68
- Meta-cognitive strategies +0.6
- Explicit teaching strategies +0.57
- Feedback +0.66

The basics of cognitive load and memory

We are not neuroscientists and this section does not go into depth about the scientific principles that underpin cognitive load theory or memory or indeed the functionality of the brain. What we do here is outline the key principles that we, as educators, need to consider and have a basic understanding of if we are to support the best learning in our classrooms.

Cognitive load relates to the amount of information we can hold in our working memory at any one time. Processing new information results in cognitive load. Working memory has limited capacity and as such we need to ensure that we don't overload with tasks or activities that don't directly facilitate or contribute to learning. First let's review what happens with information. When information enters our brain there is first a 'filtering' of sensory information. This information is essentially all the things that are going on around us at any point in time and is, put simply, how our brain processes sensory input from multiple sensory modalities; vision, auditory, tactile stimulation, olfaction, and gustation (otherwise known as sight, hearing, touch, smell, and taste). Sensory processing is where the brain filters out useful sensory information from the many thousands of stimuli present in the external environment, so that only useful information is sent to the working memory. Essentially the brain is filtering out unimportant details. A very basic example is people who live next to a train track. When you live next to a train track or even on a flight path, after a period of living in the property you don't notice the noise from the trains or the planes. Visitors might, however, be acutely aware of such noises. You are using sensory filtering. In the classroom some students are able to filter out background information, such as the noise of the projector, footsteps in the hall, students turning pages, the lawnmower outside, birds singing in the trees and yet for other students they are unable to filter this out. Often those students with autism are acutely aware of environmental stimuli and filter sensory information to differing degrees which is something we must consider with our learning environment. Being acutely aware of some stimuli can lead to distraction, anxiety, difficulties listening to a task while for example writing or reading or over focusing on a key aspect. Students with ADHD also show deficits in their working memory (Kasper et al., 2012). While approximately 10% of individuals have weak working memory, 'the estimates of the percentage of weak working memory in students with specific learning disorders including dyslexia ranges from 20 to 50 percent' (<https://dyslexiada.org/working-memory-the-engine-for-learning/>). The effect size for ADHD is -0.9 without treatment and +0.30 with treatment drugs (Visible Learning Plus, June 2019). It is important therefore as practitioners that we revisit the strategies we have in place to support learners with additional needs in our classroom, paying particular attention to the impact on and development of working memory. Our strategies must be underpinned by working memory.

Activity 1:
Next time you are in your classroom make a conscious note to stop and listen. Listen to all the things that are going on in the background that you usually filter out. Think about how those things might impact on a hypersensitive learner. Can you control any of these inputs? Can, for example, the buzzing on your projector or computer be fixed?

Fundamentally, we could argue filtering is what impacts our perception and so this plays an important part in learning because we have no doubt found ourselves in the position of one learner seeing something one way and another a different way. We attempt to explain and 'they still don't get it'. We have to acknowledge 'perception' and at this point think about adding back to the filtered information in order to support learning and this is why we must ensure we do not create sensory overload. Look at Image 4.1, what do you see? The beautiful woman or the old witch? The image is of course the same but how our brain perceives it may be different to how another person perceives the same image. To get someone to see something differently we need to pinpoint key features for them (reference point identification), and we need to be very clear how that connects to the next feature. When I saw this image many years ago as a child,

The learning cycle

Ambiguous object

Do you see the young lady or the old woman?

Image 4.1 A famous perceptual illusion in which the brain switches between seeing an old lady or a young woman. This image is believed to have been adapted by W. E. Hill and published in Puck Magazine in 1915 (Hill, 1915) although the image is believed to have originated from an anonymous German postcard in 1888

I could not see the beautiful woman at all. All I could see was the witch. It took someone to clearly show me how key points on the image link together to become the beautiful woman. This can be much the same with a learner's perception in your classroom. Your job is to identify those connections to allow them to 'see'.

The Atkinson–Shiffrin model is a model of memory (Atkinson & Shiffrin, 1968) which describes memory as having three separate components: sensory memory, working or short-term memory, and long-term memory. Sensory memory is where sensory information enters the brain and is either forgotten or moves to working memory. Working or short-term memory is where this information is held, and it receives information from the sensory memory and retrieves information from the long-term memory. Long-term memory is where we hold indefinitely information which has been rehearsed. This is summarized in Figure 4.3.

Different types of memory

Episodic memory is where we store information and events from the recent past, for example, what we did yesterday. Procedural memory is the store of knowledge we gain over time, such as driving a car or riding a bike. It is our habits and our memory for skills. If you haven't ridden a bike for 20 years, it might take 5

The learning cycle

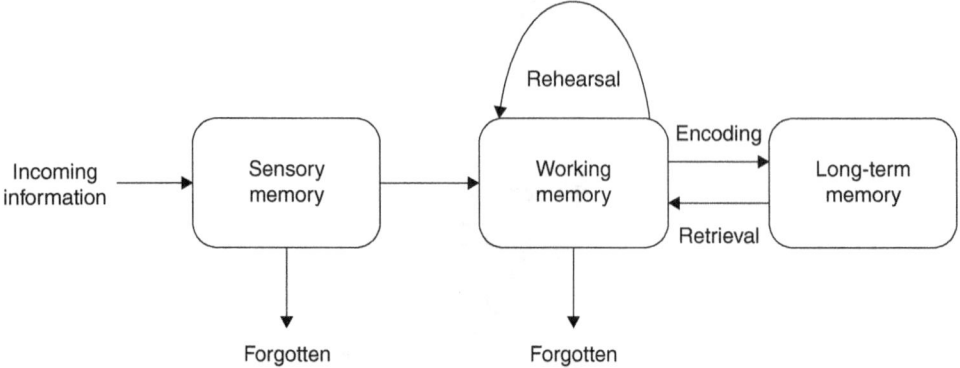

Figure 4.3 Information Processing Model (referenced from Atkinson and Shiffrin, 1968)

minutes or so for you to get 'used to it' but you will remember and ultimately be able to ride the bike (automation). Semantic memory is the store of knowledge gained over a lifetime, for example, when we read our ability to understand the meaning of the words, spellings, and how we pronounce different words. You reading this book is using semantic memory.

Working memory

Working memory is crucial for learning and is a process – it is not 'rote learning', which involves the passive *memorization* of static information. Working memory in contrast allows us, over short periods of time, to hold and manipulate information mentally. For example, remembering a question long enough for us to formulate a response (remember the time when you were in an interview and forgot the question!) or performing mental arithmetic. Information is processed through the working memory, but it has limited capacity and can be overloaded. The duration of working memory is typically limited to seconds and adults can only hold 6 or 7 pieces of information in working memory and a young adult 3 to 5 pieces. When information is lost from working memory it cannot be retrieved. We will work on the basis that an average person can hold only approximately 4 chunks of information in their working memory (Cowan, 2010).

Students with weak working memory may (<https://dyslexiada.org/working-memory-the-engine-for-learning/>):

- Perform below average in some or all areas of learning.

The learning cycle

- Have difficulty with complex problems.
- Have trouble with tasks that have more than one step.
- Stop working because they have lost track of what they are supposed to do.
- Frequently engage in daydreaming.
- Lack skills in planning and organization.
- Have trouble remembering all the steps in oral direction.
- Have trouble thinking and doing at the same time.
- Appear highly distracted and inattentive but not impulsive or hyperactive.
- Demonstrate low self-esteem.
- Have relationships with peers but have difficulty following conversation in a group.

The amount of information we can hold in our working memory coupled with a consideration of sensory processing is critical for lesson design and implementation.

Long-term memory

Learning requires information to be committed to long-term memory. Long-term memory is where we store our life's memories and information that we have acquired. If learning has been successful, then students should be able to store that information and retrieve it effectively, 'if nothing has changed in the long-term memory nothing has been learned' (Kirschner et al., 2016: 77).

Storing information in the long-term memory depends on how well we have managed and utilized our working memory. Information is stored in the long-term memory as schemas. A schema organizes elements of information according to how they will be used. Schemas can be simple or highly complex structures. The limitations of our working memory can be overcome by schema construction and automation. Automation occurs after extensive practice (Sweller et al., 1998). For example, if I ask you to remember the following sequence of numbers 1,9,1,4,1,9,1,8,1,9,3,9,1,9,4,5 as a series of individual numbers (16 discrete items to remember) you will most likely struggle to remember them one minute later or indeed the next day. If, however, we re-write these as 1914, 1918, 1939, 1945

The learning cycle

you will have 4 items to remember and written as 'dates' your brain is more likely to remember them. Further make a connection with the start and end of World Wars and you are highly likely to remember these at any point in the future. This is because you have a schema already constructed in your long-term memory. Of course, this depends on your level of 'expert'. A year 2 student (6/7 year old) will be a novice and will not have a schema development linking dates and World Wars. This exemplifies the importance of prior knowledge. If, however, I asked a child to remember the letters e-l-b-a-t as 5 discrete items and then compare to t-a-b-l-e as one item the child would be able to visualize and reference and therefore recall.

Working memory supports the organization of the schema or tells our brain where to put things in the long-term memory and looks for connections with prior learning. How it makes these connections is the degree of organization. Think of a wardrobe. A well-organized wardrobe is based on a 'system of organization' and may store all the shirts together, all the trousers together or alternatively might use a colour-coded storage system. This makes it easy to find items. A disorganized wardrobe where clothes are 'thrown in' in any way is not ordered and it is more challenging to find things and appears chaotic and stressful to the brain.

Our working memory helps us store things in the correct place in our long-term memory so that we 'know where to look' when we need the information, rather like a very complicated filing system. Connections are important, for example, if I ask you what you did yesterday and then what you did last year on the same date, most likely you will remember yesterday very clearly (short-term memory) but you will not remember exactly what you did on the same day a year ago. In fact, it is highly likely you will have absolutely no recollection at all. Why? Because there is no reference point. Now if I link a further piece of information 'birthdays', your brain makes a connection and goes to a specific area of your brain or filing cabinet titled 'birthdays'. Most likely you can remember something about your birthday last year; the presents you received, the cake, who you celebrated with or where you went. Clear connections are essential when we talk about developing learning and most important memory. Abstract pieces of information will be retained short term but will not be retained in the long term. Thus, making the learning redundant.

Information moves from working memory to long-term memory through practice and rehearsal by encoding information which can be done using different cognitive activities. It is important to avoid cognitive overload or encoding cannot happen or cannot happen effectively which leads to misconceptions, misunderstanding, and a confused learner. Automation is the process by which you complete activities with minimal conscious effort. When you get in your car and drive to work, for example, your brain acts on automation and looks to your long-term memory and schema and you effectively act on 'auto-pilot'.

'Learning to read is a good example of schema construction and automation. Children begin to learn to read by constructing schemas for squiggles on a page – letters. These simple schemas for letters are used to construct higher-order schemas when they are combined into words' (Sweller et al., 1998). The authors go on to say that sentences are formed from the combination of these words through schemas and that reading requires minimal conscious effort as practice becomes more extensive.

Cognitive load

There are three types of cognitive load: intrinsic, extraneous, and germane.

Intrinsic load is related directly to the complexity of the material and the prior knowledge of the learner. The impact of intrinsic load is therefore dependent on the degree of expertise the learner has. It would include process-driven calculations, for example (see Image 4.2).

To make intrinsic load positive we must focus on the level of expertise of our students. The maths problem in Image 4.2 would be easy for a year 11 student ('expert') but complex for a year 3 student ('novice').

Extraneous load is negative and results in high cognitive load and does not contribute to learning. This is where a learner is presented with a problem and then left to 'Figure it out' with little prior input. It creates misconceptions as the focus is on solving and not learning a process or underpinning concept. It does

$$\frac{3x}{y} - 1 = m$$
$$\times y \left(\frac{3x}{y} = m + 1 \right) \times y$$
$$\div 3 \left(3x = y(m + 1) \right) \div 3$$
$$x = \frac{y(m + 1)}{3}$$

Image 4.2 An illustration of a mathematical calculation which involves a stepwise process to solve for x

The learning cycle

not support the construction of schema or automation and is linked to how the material is presented.

Germane load contributes directly to learning and is a positive effect. The 'I do, we do, you do' cycle is an example of this where we explicitly model and support with worked examples. It develops schema and automation as we focus on the 'how' before we give learners similar problems to tackle. Germane load supports information processing.

As teachers this simply means we need to maximize germane load, minimize extraneous load and manage intrinsic load.

What is dual coding?

Dual coding forms one part of a wider theory known as the cognitive theory of multimedia learning or CTML. It is where different stimuli are used to help learners to encode information in their brains supporting later retrieval. Visual and verbal are the two main types of stimuli typically used in the classroom where we provide two different representations of the information to help students better learn. For example, combining words and visuals: diagrams, graphic organizers, images. In biology if we only describe the parts of the cell verbally to students then the information appears abstract without the combination of a diagram. The pictorial representation allows students to link the information. Dual coding, however, can be implemented poorly and an example of this is 'too much teacher talk' creating an environment for abstract learning.

Visual and verbal information is processed differently in the brain as simplified in Figure 4.4. Primarily dual coding involves us thinking about how we deliver material in our lessons and supports us simplifying complex ideas. In 1971 Allan Paivio used the idea that the formation of mental images aids learning. According to Paivio, there are two ways a person could expand on learned material: verbal associations and visual imagery. As practitioners we need to decide on the appropriate visual and determine if it is relevant. A visual can be an image or a text. The visual element needs to be carefully selected and accurate. An inaccurate diagram reinforces misconceptions. Referring to the section on sensory input, remember when you design your slides to think about the background and potential sensory overload; keeping the slides plain and using font such as Ariel is best. This supports all learners but is especially beneficial for those learners with additional needs who struggle with sensory overload.

The learning cycle

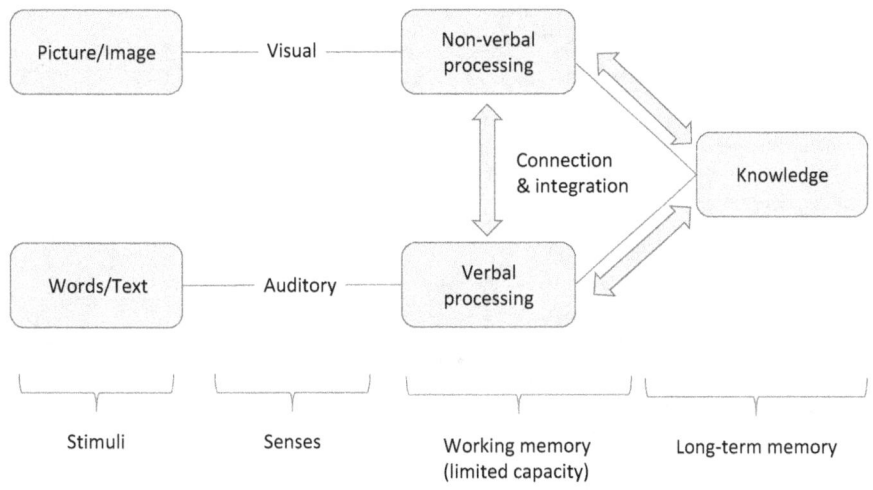

Figure 4.4 A summary Figure based on Allan Paivio's 1971 dual-coding theory

When you use and explain a diagram ensure you are focused on specific knowledge, don't go into extensive complicated prose or off on a tangent but use simple, short sentences that contain key information. In general, diagrams are best explained verbally. If we have a slide with both the diagram and explanatory text we create high cognitive load with two visual inputs, for example text and an image/diagram. This is illustrated in Figure 4.5. Remember while dual coding is a powerful memory technique, we must not create diagrams or visual representation for the sake of it. Text alone is a visual representation that can be spoken through and is highly effective for learners. Timelines, comic strips, story boards, data in tables, Venn diagrams, flow charts, graphic organizers are all excellent tools for dual coding as are many revision techniques.

The learning cycle

The curriculum should be thought of as a continuum but not simply a linear progression, more one that resembles a complex web of interleaving knowledge points. For effective memory retention this knowledge must be pre-determined (identified in the curriculum for each composite) and be specific. This way we will support effective use of the working memory and long-term memory storage allowing students to make connections. Knowledge really develops when connections are made with facts, and when we use consistent underlying

The learning cycle

(a)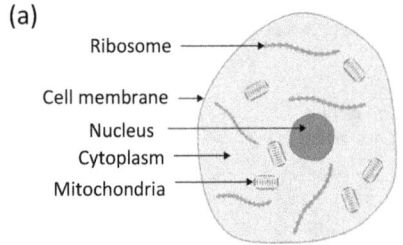

(b)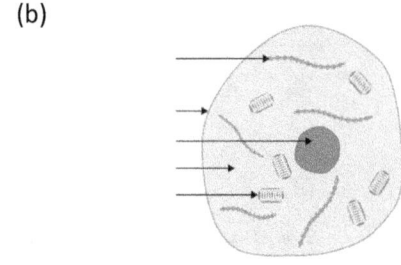

The four key components of most animal cells are:
- **Nucleus** - this contains the genetic material (DNA) of the organism and controls the cell's activities.
- **Cytoplasm** - the liquid that makes up most of the cell in which chemical reactions happen. This is mainly water.
- **Cell membrane** - a flexible outer layer that surrounds the cell and controls which substances can pass into and out from it.
- **Mitochondria** - tiny parts of cells floating in the cytoplasm where energy is released from glucose from food. The mitochondria, found in the cell cytoplasm, are where most happens.

Figure 4.5 Slide (a) has both the image of an animal cell and the text which the teacher also reads out to the class. This creates overload. In (b) there is only the image of the animal cell and the teacher reads the definition for students to then label (images of the cell from Steve Cymro/Shutterstock.com)

concepts linked to each other as our foundations combined with retrieval practice. The learning cycle is the process by which our students acquire, develop and apply, and recall knowledge. It is therefore critical that in our composites we pinpoint what this specific knowledge is and that we use end-point planning to ensure that our students develop this knowledge over the course of a lesson or series of lessons (determined by the length of the composite, as discussed in Chapter 2), keeping in mind the magic number of four (cognitive load).

The learning cycle we will explore in this chapter focuses on how we develop our lessons through the most common lesson style and is illustrated in Figure 4.6.

1. The start of the lesson.
2. The cycle in the main (of which there may be one main cycle or multiple cycles): *I do, we do, you do & review.*
3. The plenary.

The learning cycle

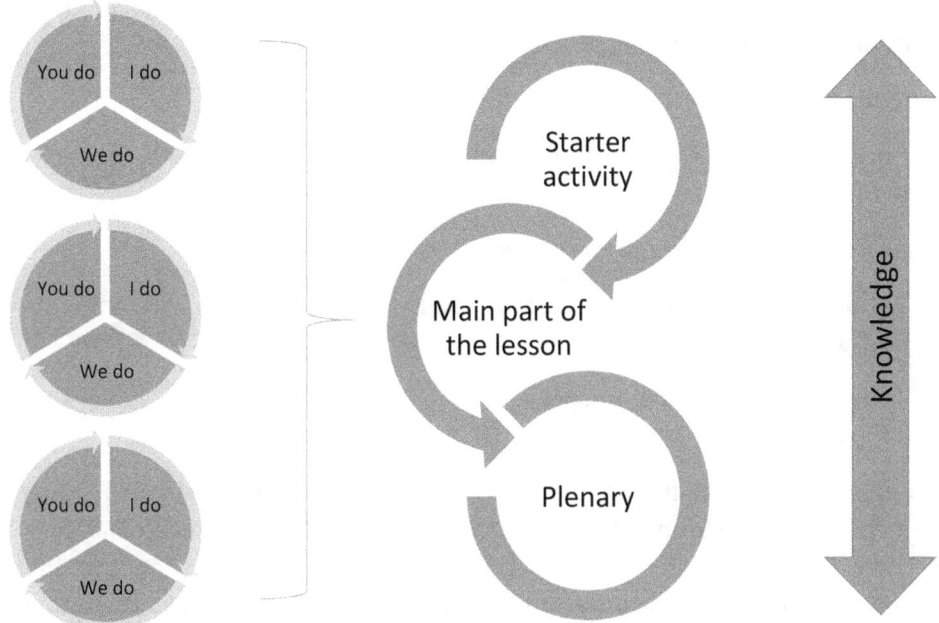

Figure 4.6 An illustration of the learning cycle within the common '3-part' cycle

The start of the lesson and the big question

As discussed in Chapter 2 each component and composite will identify powerful knowledge and this is why investing time in the quality of your curriculum is so important. If the knowledge is vague and not specific then it will be much more difficult for you to create your lesson because there may be ambiguity and this then creates drift in lesson planning. Link this to cognitive load where the working memory can only hold a small amount of information and we lead to poor retention; to avoid the redundancy effect specificity is a critical component of curriculum development.

One of the most common things we see at the start of the lesson is a slide which states 'what are we learning today' or 'our leaning objectives/outcomes', for example.

Typical examples of learning objectives are given below:

- I will be able to expand double brackets and apply this to problem solving.
- I will know how to describe the layers of the rainforest.

- I will be able to explain the difference in reactivity as we go down group 1 in the periodic table.
- I will know the parts of the plant cell.

Now put yourself in the mindset of one of your students and ask yourself the following questions:

- 'What does this **mean to the student**?'
- 'Is this more for **me as a teacher**, in other words a tick list of content we will get through?'
- 'What is the **learning purpose**, do we do this because we have always done it?'

Through the time spent researching and working with teachers and students on curriculum development we would argue learning outcomes/objectives at the start of the lesson are more for the teacher. When we translate this into a purposeful question it becomes more for the students as it allows them to add meaning to their learning and creates a meaningful purpose to the acquisition of knowledge 'success'. I refer to this as the Big Question (Bartlett, 2015a). A Big Question is a question which asks students to apply their knowledge or learning (Bartlett, 2015a) and is carefully crafted to recall key knowledge. The direct 'before' and 'after' comparison develops metacognition.

If a student can answer the big question at the end of the lesson and they could not do this at the start (which of course, if skillfully planned, is the aim) – or alternatively that they have developed their answer to the Big Question by the end of the lesson allowing them to respond with specific knowledge – then students will feel they have 'learned' something. This is about learning mindset. What we do next to deepen that learning and ensure it is not a 'one off' that we tick as completed relies heavily on the curriculum itself and whether our curriculum builds on the foundations of prior knowledge, learning, and the application of skills and in making connections.

Examples of Big Questions are discussed in detail in Bartlett, 2015a, however, in relation to the learning objectives stated above Big Questions might be:

1. Which has the greater area (refer to Image 4.3)? Are there parameters on the value of x?
2. Why are many animals in the tropical rainforest nocturnal?

The learning cycle

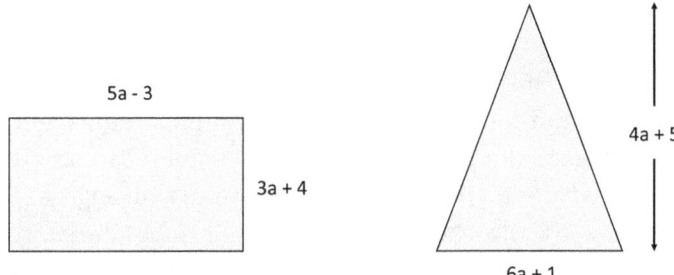

Image 4.3 Which has the greater area?

3. Why does caesium explode when exposed to air more rigorously than lithium?

4. What part of plant cells gives them their crunch?

The quality of your curriculum couldn't be more important for defining the Big Question and below we look at some examples of

- The component
- The knowledge
- The learning outcomes (an aid for the teacher)
- The Big Question

If we consider a component based on the properties of the group 1 alkali metals. The specific knowledge that we want students to know may include that reactivity increases as we go down the group because the atoms get larger and the outer electrons get further away from the nucleus meaning that the attraction between the nucleus and the single outer electron gets weaker and it is therefore more easily 'lost'. The learning outcome might be that 'students know and can explain why reactivity increases down the group 1 metals'. A big question might be 'why does caesium explode when exposed to air more rigorously than lithium?'.

Activity 2:
Take a lesson or series of lessons and identify a big question. Identify up to 4 chunks of information required to answer this. How does this sharpen your focus on the component knowledge and the input or process factors that contribute to learning and the development of schema?

The learning cycle

The starter activity

What comes first sets the tone. Imagine reading a book, if the first chapter is poor you most likely put the book down and never pick it up again. If our stater activity does not engage the brain – and this does not mean an all-singing, all-dancing starter activity – then students will naturally disengage. Boredom has an effect size of -0.49 (Hattie, 2009). Engagement is about creating a culture for thinking and the skill is pitching this at just the right level. You know your class best and you will know the hinge point for too easy (students switch off) and too challenging (students switch off). Teacher estimates of achievement has an effect size of +1.29 (Hattie, 2009). Success is a really powerful motivator and we need to capture this. Motivation has an effect size of +0.42 and achieving motivation and approach +0.44 (Hattie, 2009). Avoid using generic lessons and if you do use pre-planned lessons always review and tailor to the needs of your class. We are all individuals, and in your class, you have 30 different students, they may have a similar ability level but they are all individuals – think back to the discussion about learning needs and memory. Having the same test score does not mean two people learn in the same way. People have different prior knowledge and different prior experiences. You must know your students and understand their needs. Our planning needs to reflect the differences. Cognitive load theory allows us to optimize the impact of our implementation by carefully selecting techniques which support learning.

There are many different starter activities that we can use and as practitioners you will no doubt have tried many different activities over time. We draw reference to Bartlett, 2015a, for lots of different ideas for types of starter activities themselves; here, however, we focus on knowledge and memory, and this can be applied to different activities which we will exemplify in this section.

The simplest and yet probably most powerful activity for improving retention is the knowledge retrieval starter. This focuses on improving memory and developing schema, but I add a proviso here – only if done well. 'Cognitive scientists think of deep learning – or what you might call 'learning for understanding' – as the ability to organize discrete pieces of knowledge into a larger schema of understanding' (Meta & Fine, 2019).

A carefully crafted knowledge retrieval starter begins this process. To the outsider looking in this may simply look like a 'quiz' or series of questions on a topic, to you and your learners they must be skillfully designed to test the individual student's ability to recall and apply. A knowledge recall activity should not simply be a set of questions from previous lessons but one that draws on the prior knowledge that links to the lesson (refer to the concept of inter-leaving and spaced learning). Using retrieval practice helps learners to improve their memory by focusing on what they need to learn, not overloading the working memory with irrelevant information (the redundancy effect). Remember that while retrieval practice improves memory if we haven't encoded the information effectively in the first place then recall will be limited. We can also utilize spaced learning through the knowledge retrieval starter where we distribute learning and retrieval opportunities over a longer period rather than placing them at a particular point in time, for example, the start of the next lesson instead creating a 'concentrated' pool of short-term memory retrieval. We can build in recall from last lesson, a lesson a week ago or 2 weeks ago. A point to note, and one often overlooked, is that retrieval quizzes do not need to be at the start of the lesson and can be placed where you consider key points for learning. One reason we often place them at the start is as a check in to note any gaps or possible misconceptions that may impact the lesson and also because they are quite a 'settling' activity. As we increase memory strength through carefully spaced retrieval – where we recall from previous lessons over a period – we can identify opportunities for reteach and curriculum content review.

Literacy remains a key focus for learning and those students with strong literacy skills arguably achieve higher in their examinations. It is therefore important that you encourage students to respond to a knowledge retrieval exercise in full sentences. Using Figure 4.7 as an example we can see that simply

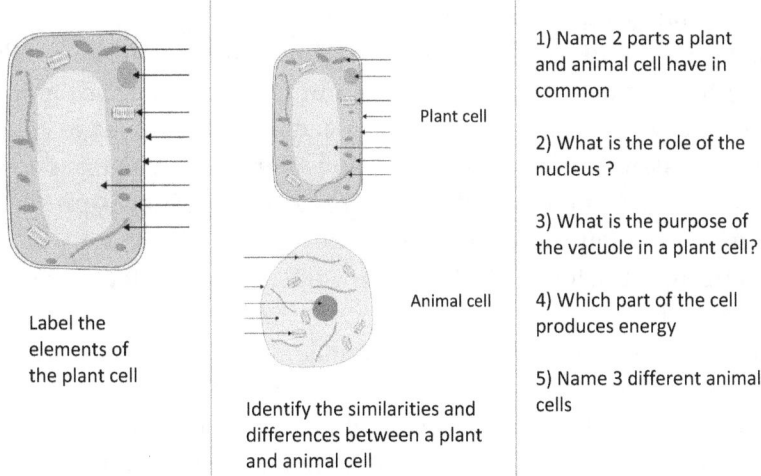

Figure 4.7 Examples of different starter activities based on the cell (images of the cell from Steve Cymro/Shutterstock.com)

labelling the cell is an exercise in basic memory recall whereas the questions involve a deeper thought process. This again allows a longer 'thinking time' and will support memory retention. To avoid sensory overload, ask the question once, repeat this and then allow a period of silence for students to process and recall. We are often uncomfortable as teachers with periods of silence and for some reason feel the need to fill them, hence we start talking. Next time you are teaching create an opportunity for silence and allow the silence to happen; periods of silence feel much longer – count slowly to 10 in your head and you will see. Having the question on the board does not cause sensory overload – the brain processes auditory and visual (the written text in this case) in two different areas (refer back to dual coding). Remember if you are talking about other things while the students are answering the questions it will be harder for them to 'focus' as you are providing another sensory input. Our students with learning needs such as autism and ADHD will not be able to filter out this sensory information and thus creating sensory overload.

Other activities can of course serve the same purpose. The aim of this chapter is not to explore all the different types of starter activity, but to get you thinking about the key questions to ask yourself about the starter activity you choose. We will address how a small sample can be used to achieve the same end point. Retrieval practice is not simply a series of short answer fact questions which students work through, the questions need to be designed to pinpoint specific knowledge. Other powerful activities include: pair matching and card sorts, true or false statements, labelling diagrams, comparing images, multiple choice questions and many more similar activities.

Pair matching and card sorting activities (an example is shown in Figure 4.8) for instance can be a simple but effective exercise and promote working memory, but again the activity needs to be knowledge specific and enable you to assess prior knowledge and therefore in many ways acts as a baseline. Retrieval practice, through whatever medium it presents, helps students to strengthen their memory on key concepts but we need to pitch it at the appropriate level of challenge; too easy and it will not increase memory strength.

Open-ended tasks need more careful thought because there is the danger of drift and open-ended tasks at the start of a lesson take more careful managing to ensure that you achieve the desired end point. What we mean by this is that they can allow a student to not be specific enough and if the purpose is knowledge retrieval, then we require a specific piece of knowledge recall. Reviewing an open-ended task can therefore be quite challenging as students will all have

$x^2 - 64$	$(x + 7)(x + 3)$
$x^2 + 4x - 21$	$(x - 5)(x + 4)$
$x^2 - 10x + 21$	$(x - 8)^2$
$x^2 - 16x + 64$	$(x + 7)(x + 3)$
$x^2 - x - 20$	$(x - 7)(x - 3)$
$x^2 + 10x + 21$	$(x - 8)(x + 8)$

Figure 4.8 An example of a pair matching exercise which involves the retrieval of process knowledge

a different output, whereas simple knowledge retrieval allows for more precise benchmarking. An example of an open-ended task in the main part of the lesson would be investigation or a piece of extended writing in English. In mathematics, for example, the jellybean investigation is where students investigate how many jellybeans could fill the room. In History students may be asked to write an essay on 'Life in Elizabethan England'. For the starter activity an open-ended task could be 'describe the process of nuclear fusion'. This is a short recall task but is allowing students the opportunity to 'write more' and can cause drift and non-specific knowledge. Key is to ensure students can pinpoint the powerful knowledge which is useful preparation for longer questions in examinations. If, for example, you wish to develop paragraph response writing then you could specify the knowledge or key points that you want students to include. This scaffolds the knowledge. It will be the responses to these points that would allow benchmarking of knowledge retrieval.

Whichever style of starter activity you choose to use as knowledge retrieval it is essential that you review the activity. This further discussion and auditory input promotes memory. Students can identify areas of development and this self-monitoring of learning can lead to strategies for improvement.

Learning in the main

> I hear and I forget. I see and I remember. I do and I understand.
>
> (Confucius)

Possibly an additional sentence of 'I hear and I see and I remember' and Confucius has the principle for dual coding. The main part of the lesson is where we introduce new knowledge and is where new learning happens. Modelling and scaffolding are crucial components of the main part of the lesson (herein referred to simply as the main) and are skills which every practitioner needs to develop.

When done well they have the power to transform learning and the step-by-step approach can reduce cognitive load (Sweller, 2016). When done badly they may create a passive environment and it is that balance that we need to achieve which is where our knowledge of the learners in our classroom is absolutely critical and why we must avoid taking a lesson 'off the shelf' simply because it is on a given topic and we must always ensure we carefully tailor the lesson to make it suitable for our audience. Hattie summarizes the learning cycle:

> The teacher decides the learning intentions and success criteria, makes them transparent to the students, demonstrates them by modelling, evaluates if they understand what they have been told by checking for understanding, and retelling them what they have been told by tying it all together with closure.
>
> (Hattie, 2009, p. 206)

Cognitive load theory and learning in the main

Cognitive load theory and the development of schema supports the 'I do, we do, you do' cycle (germane load). We must, however, consider the level of expertise of the student and where possible ensure we are connecting with prior conceptions and developing schema, as opposed to learning something entirely new. Go back to what we said about perception and individuality. How a learner connects schema is also outside of the control of the teacher and unique to the student themselves. Therefore, in the 'I do' phase we must be as explicit as possible and avoid the redundancy effect where the learner's limited working memory is directed to unnecessary or redundant information. Modelling is an example of the *worked example effect* (Sweller, 2016).

The worked example effect
In the worked example effect we take a step-by-step approach to model the process. An example often cited is that in mathematics, for example, solving a mathematical equation as illustrated in Image 4.4.

In this example, we carefully take the learner through each step and we reinforce the importance of the development of the mathematical sequence. We

$$8x - 7 = 3x + 4$$
$$+7 \quad\quad +7$$
$$8x = 3x + 11$$
$$-3x \quad -3x$$
$$\div 5 \left(\begin{array}{c} 5x = 11 \\ x = \dfrac{11}{5} \end{array} \right) \div 5$$

Image 4.4 A step-by-step approach to solving equations. Step 1: subtract 7 from both sides (carefully aligning numbers). Step 2: Subtract 3x from both sides. Step 3: Solve by dividing through by 5

need, however, to be mindful that the 'method' that we choose is one which actually reduces cognitive load rather than adds to it.

The split attention effect

We must be careful with how we present information so that we do not create a split attention effect. This has a negative impact on cognitive load as it requires the learner to process two separate pieces of information simultaneously, in order, to make sense of the activity. For example, where a separate piece of text is required to interpret a diagram. To minimize this, we need to consider where we can combine sources into one piece of information. An example given by Sweller (2016) is the geometry problem. Typically, in mathematics this involves a diagram and then a piece of text. Sweller notes 'if a geometry statement mentions Angle ABC, learners have to note the angle and find it on the diagram. Until the statement and the diagram have been mentally integrated, neither can make any sense' (Sweller, 2016). In other words, the learner has to mentally integrate and process two sources. Sweller states 'if instead the statements are placed on the diagram or had arrows indicating the relations between each statement and the diagram, the worked example is physically integrated and working memory resources do not have to be expected to integrate the two sources of information' (Sweller, 2016).

In Figure 4.9 the learner doesn't actually need the diagram to find the value of one angle in a regular pentagon (as each angle is 540/5 = 108 degrees). Simply knowing the shape is regular and that we are finding one angle is enough information.

What's interesting though if you look at exam papers is that often the text is separate from the diagram and so we must build our learners to be able to

The learning cycle

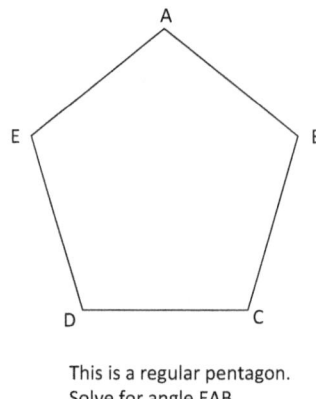

This is a regular pentagon.
Solve for angle EAB

Figure 4.9 Finding the angle in a regular pentagon

complete such problems and to ensure they can independently integrate the text and diagram. This develops as the learner's expertise develops and we should introduce and build to this slowly. This may be over a single lesson or over the course of two or three lessons.

When you look at the problems you are using and presenting through your worked example or in the 'we do' and 'you do' phase, it is very important to reference the split attention effect, otherwise you may find yourself in a position where the worked example does not have the positive outcome you planned and you have instead created extraneous cognitive load.

The modality and the transient effect

The modality effect provides an alternative to physically integrating sources of information (Sweller, 2016). It is where we use both auditory and visual input. For example, in Figure 4.5, or Figure 4.7 we could remove the text (written form) and simply 'say' the statements or questions having only the diagram – the 'visual' - displayed on the board. This links to dual coding and we increase working memory capacity by using the two different channels, however, we must be careful not to over complicate the spoken material or go off on a tangent. The spoken material needs to be concise and simple (think 'step-by-step'). This is important because once we have said the *words* they 'disappear' and are replaced by the next thing that we say. Therefore, between each simple statement (removing any redundant information) we must allow processing time. A long, complicated statement will decrease working memory.

The redundancy effect

Unnecessary information overloads the memory. We are often very good storytellers as teachers and while this may engage the learner we are actually providing redundant information and impacting on working memory. Consider the example given by Sweller (2016) in relation to the heart. The statement 'blood flows from the left ventricle to the aorta' is redundant information as this can be clearly seen from the diagram itself.

The written statement in Figure 4.10 creates extraneous cognitive load – we are processing two separate inputs. Figure 4.10 integrates this onto one diagram, one source of cognitive input. We may, however, choose to emphasize this using auditory input. Therefore, we should give careful consideration to ensuring that our diagrams are not adding to cognitive load. A further example is shown in Figures 4.11a and 4.11b.

Techniques to develop learning

There are many techniques we use to develop learning and in this section we outline a sample.

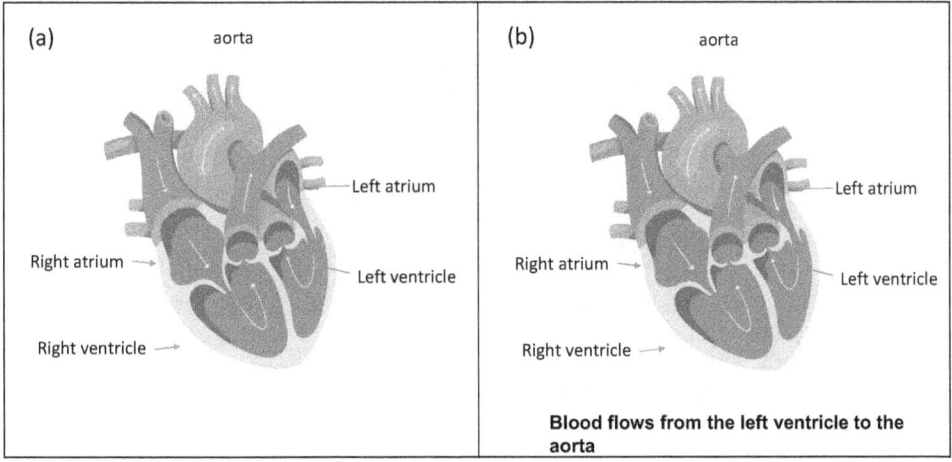

Figure 4.10 Two diagrams with the same information. On diagram (b) the statement 'blood flows from the left ventricle to the aorta' is redundant (images of the heart from Katalin Macevics/Shutterstock.com)

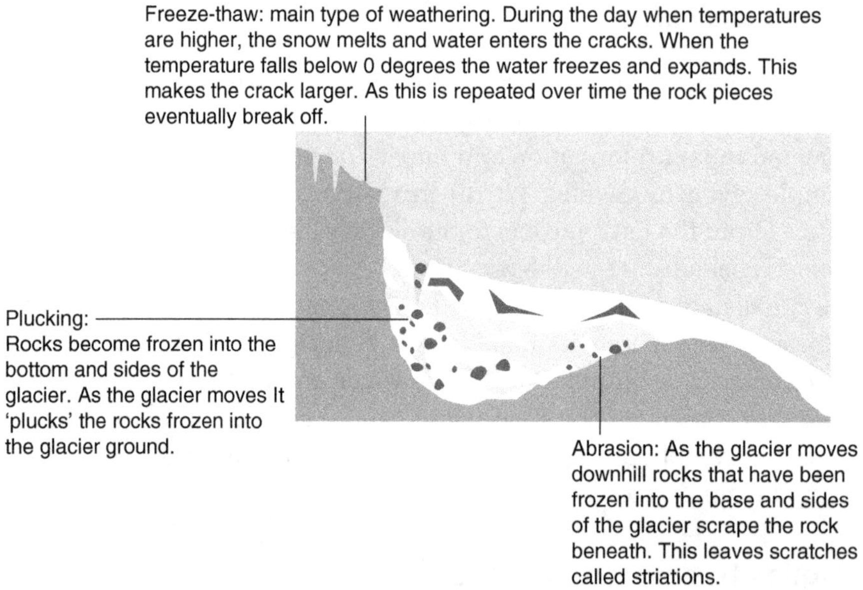

The learning cycle

Freeze-thaw: main type of weathering. During the day when temperatures are higher, the snow melts and water enters the cracks. When the temperature falls below 0 degrees the water freezes and expands. This makes the crack larger. As this is repeated over time the rock pieces eventually break off.

Plucking: Rocks become frozen into the bottom and sides of the glacier. As the glacier moves It 'plucks' the rocks frozen into the glacier ground.

Abrasion: As the glacier moves downhill rocks that have been frozen into the base and sides of the glacier scrape the rock beneath. This leaves scratches called striations.

Figure 4.11a The diagram here showing the glacial process creates extraneous cognitive load through the visual image and the complex text. If this is then talked through by the teacher it creates an additional sensory input. Diagram and content adapted from BBC Bitesize

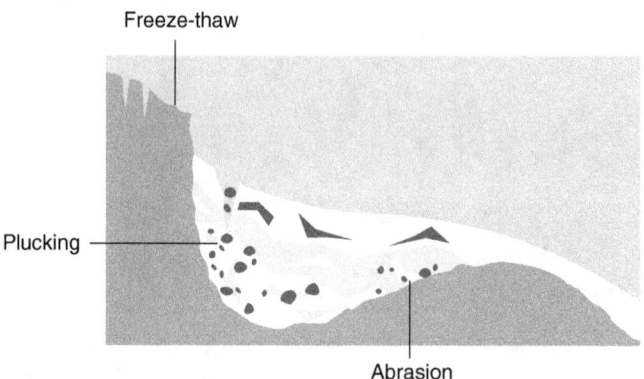

Figure 4.11b The diagram here showing the glacial process provides a clear image which is simple and reduces input. Each part of the process can then be explained by the teacher. Diagram and content adapted from BBC Bitesize

Modelling

Limited working memory, particularly in the novice student, can result in cognitive overload quite quickly. Modelling takes a step-by-step approach and teaches students the process. Once this is mastered and enters long-term memory capacity is created within the working memory and students can apply this to problem solving. How we deliver the 'I do' does not mean the only input is from the teacher and time and time again I observe this pattern and I see students who become passive and disengaged. Quite the opposite is needed at this stage; the 'I do' phase needs to be highly interactive and is where skilful questioning is needed.

> Tell me and I forget, teach me and I may remember, involve me and I learn.
> (Benjamin Franklin)

Auditory and visual input typically support memory in this stage. As students become less novice and more expert, we can reduce the level of scaffolding needed to support process development.

We should note that the level of expertise that the learner has is important to be considered as we need to gain a balance. Too much scaffolding for the expert learner becomes less and less effective and ultimately becomes counterproductive and leads to the expertise reversal effect which is an exception to the worked example or scaffolded approach (Leslie et al. 2012; Pachman et al., 2013; Yeung et al., 1998). While cognitive load theory supports heavy scaffolding for the novice student, it also supports the gradual incorporation of more independent problem-solving tasks as students gain expertise. Balance is the key, and we only gain balance by knowing our students. Too much and there is no encoding (misconceptions) and too little and there is no cognitive processing, meaning no learning has taken place. It is worth noting that we are not advocating a teacher talk and students approach, rather the modelling phase equips students with the skills to access the lesson, our role is to determine how much input our students need.

We will have carefully considered the sequence of learning and the Big Question helps to sharpen and focus our thinking, identifying the specific knowledge and processes required and eliminating unnecessary information. 'Most people assume that providing learners with additional information is at worst, harmless and might be beneficial. Redundancy is anything but harmless. Providing unnecessary information can be a major reason for instructional failure' (Sweller, 2016, p. 8).

The learning cycle

Often in planning teachers work backwards. If they know the 'end goal' of the lesson, then they flip the learning to ensure that their lesson develops progressively towards this creating a layered effect. Coupled with the work on cognitive load there are significant implications for teacher planning.

In English the studying of Shakespeare can create high cognitive load. The language is complex, students have to manage their understanding of the scene, interpret the poetic form and imagery and recognize underlying themes and context. This often creates high levels of challenge for the teacher but if we consider the effects of cognitive load, modelling can be developed though the decomposition of a paragraph.

For example, we may take a paragraph in the centre of the page with key information highlighted and bubbles with arrows around the outside where we synthesize the key points. As we develop this in the 'I do' phase we can progress to the 'we do' by providing a similar paragraph but with the bubbles only partially filled with sentence starters. Following a class discussion and review we move to the 'you do' as appropriate and further review. Reducing the scaffolding will support the learner to develop and support learners in analysing pieces of text.

When solving a mathematical equation, we need to develop thinking. A simple concept for students to grasp is the balance effect and for instance if we take $2 + 3 = 5$. If I subtract 1 from the left-hand side '$2 + 3 - 1$' what must I do to the right-hand side to ensure the equation is balanced? Students will immediately say '4' but it's the concept of '$5 - 1$' that needs to form the discussion. This is the foundation for algebraic processes. As shown in Figure 4.12 if we want to solve for x then we need to ensure that we have first embedded the concept of balance. As we develop the 'I do' modelling we should be involving students through careful questioning. In step 1 we may be asking the following questions:

- If the purpose is to get 'x on it's own' where might I start?

- If I add 5 to the left-hand side what must I do to the right-hand side?

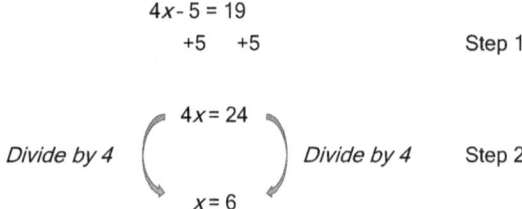

Figure 4.12 An example of an 'I do' process for solving equations

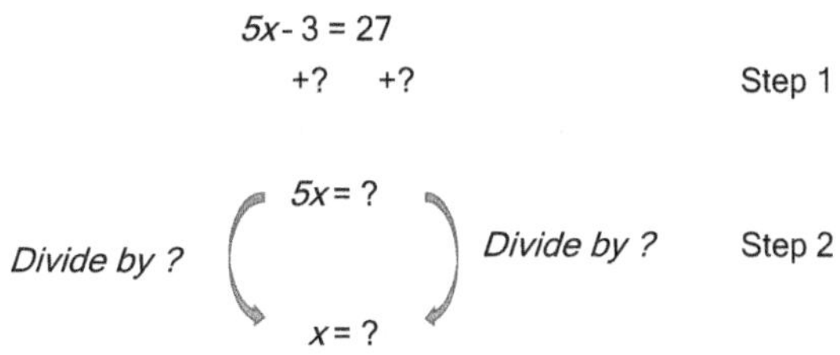

The learning cycle

$$5x - 3 = 27$$
$$+?\quad +?\qquad \text{Step 1}$$

$$\text{Divide by ?}\ \left(\begin{array}{c}5x = ?\\ \\ x = ?\end{array}\right)\ \text{Divide by ?}\qquad \text{Step 2}$$

Figure 4.13 An example of a 'we do' process for solving equations

This develops thinking. For step 2 we need to ask students 'what does $4x$ actually mean?'. Hopefully the prior knowledge is retrieved 'it means 4 times x'. Once this is clear we can discuss how we might find 'one lot of x'. This will lead to the discussion of division and if needed an analogy can be given, for example, if I bought 4 hats for £24 how would I calculate the cost of one hat?'. Discussion in the 'I do' has value to draw from prior learning.

Figure 4.13 shows how we might extend to the 'we do' and then the 'you do' can be a short series of 5 questions to solidify and check understanding and process which are reviewed through targeted questioning. Mini whiteboards can be used for the 'we do' so that there is instant visibility of any misconceptions and all student learning can be checked.

It is also critical that we build in thinking time. Far too often this is overlooked (as discussed in the section on questioning). Thinking time is critical if we are to allow students to develop schema and to embed memory. The amount of thinking time will need to be judged by you as the professional in the room and will be representative of the complexity of the problem.

Scaffolding

The amount we scaffold is determined by the level of expertise of the learner. We must remember though that we have 30 individuals in our classroom and in a mixed ability class, for example, our range may be from the novice to the more expert (in relation to the level of the group). For example, in a primary school class you may have students who can use a formal written method to multiply 2-digit or 3-digit numbers together, for example 327 x 84, and also those students who are still grappling with the basic multiplication tables or who can only multiple a 2-digit number by a single digit, for example 32 x 4. There will be a *range* and this can be more profound in mixed ability groups. Therefore, the degree of scaffolding will be different for these learners and you would focus

The learning cycle

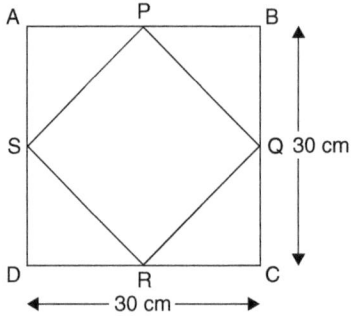

The square PQRS is made by joining the midpoints of the square ABCD.

The square ABCD has sides of length 30 cm.

Calculate the length of one side of the square PQRS.

Figure 4.14 An example of a direct question

on differentiation and ensuring that you match the most appropriate resources to the learner (Bartlett, 2015b). An example is shown in Figures 4.14 and 4.15. In Figure 4.14 the question is posed direct and in Figure 4.15 there is a layer of scaffolding to support the learner. Both questions use the same mathematical process but Figure 4.15 provides additional support. Gradually these steps become embedded into memory and the scaffolding can be withdrawn as the learner becomes more expert.

Questioning

> Who questions much, shall learn much and retain much.
>
> (Francis Bacon)

Through all phases of the lesson cycle the use of questioning is a skill that all teachers must master. Identifying the right questions and when to ask them is a skilful art and one that complements the work on cognitive load. Questioning is how we develop learning, promote thinking and how we assess learning.

Teachers ask a lot of questions, 'Teachers ask between 300-400 questions a day' (Levin & Long, 1981). It is the quality of these questions we must ensure promotes learning. When we ask a question, we should use this as a springboard for follow-on questions and I recommend at least three. This then ensures that

The learning cycle

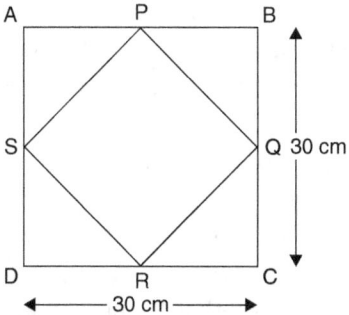

1) What is the midpoint of a line?

2) What is the length of CQ and QB?

3) Explain your answer.

4) Sketch the triangle RCQ and label the length of the sides that you know.

5) Calculate the length of RQ.

Figure 4.15 An example of the problem in Figure 4.14 but with a layer of scaffolding to support the learner

all students in the classroom will have been involved in answering more than one question. A no-hands-up approach keeps students on their toes. Different techniques support this process. The basketball technique, for example, is a well-known questioning tool where you pass the question around the classroom; the ping-pong technique is where the question comes back to you, goes to the next student, back to you and so on. Both have their merit and what both techniques do is allow the initial question to develop progressively.

Waiting time is also very important. When a teacher asks a question and then expects an immediate response then no thinking time has been allowed. When observing this is the most common pitfall of questioning and in part comes from teachers being uncomfortable with silence. Research shows that the average wait time for the response to a question is one second or less (Cotton, 1988). This is far too short and does not allow thinking time and creates cognitive stress for the student. The quality of answers will of course be reduced with a short wait time. The complexity of the question will link directly to the length of wait time needed and a lower-order question will need a shorter wait time than a higher-order question. Make a conscious effort to extend thinking time to three seconds for lower-order cognitive questions and more than this (up to seven seconds or more) for higher-order cognitive questions. If you count slowly in your head when you ask a question, then this will support the processing time for students. Higher-order cognitive questions require more wait time and increased wait time leads to higher-order cognitive discussions. Remember that you may give students longer if the question requires them to complete a short task before discussion takes place. You may also want to introduce a short pause before you respond to an answer. This allows the class to also think about the response and whether you then respond (ping pong) or whether you choose to pass it to the next student (basketball) means you will need to build in the thinking time. All of this relies on a sound culture with a safe learning environment and one where students are conditioned to high-level questioning.

Research suggests that because teachers feel that since they already use questioning in their lessons they must be doing it well, 'questioning was not an easy mediating artefact to develop partly because many teachers felt that they were already doing it and often failed to appreciate its full potential for enabling dialogue that could develop thinking' (Webb & Jones, 2009) many don't focus much attention on it or on the quality of questions that they ask. Questioning comes naturally as the course of the lesson progresses and we cannot plan for every eventuality, but when planning your lesson, we recommend you take some time to think and note down some key questions that you would like students to be able to think about or respond to and the cognitive level of these questions. The results of many studies tell us that of these questions 'approximately 60% of questions are lower order, 20% are higher order and 20% are procedural' (Cotton, 1988). There has been considerable work linking Bloom's taxonomy to questioning (Bloom, 1956). We refer you to the assessment for learning book (Bartlett, 2015a) for detailed examples. Bloom's taxonomy was updated by a research group to reflect relevance to twenty-first-century work (Anderson & Krathwohl, 2001, pp. 67–68) and the updated is based on a hierarchical structure of 6 levels which move from the lowest level of cognition (thinking) to the highest level of cognition: remembering, understanding, applying, analysing, evaluating, creating (this compares to Bloom's original taxonomy of: knowledge, comprehension, application, analysis, synthesis, and evaluation).

At the lowest level of remembering we simply ask students to recall facts. For example, sentence stems such as:

- What is…
- What is the…

- How many…
- What are the…
- Who was it that…
- Can you name…

As we progress to applying, we ask students to take the information they already know and apply it to a problem using the process they have learned. For example, sentence stems such as:

- How would you demonstrate…
- What would result if we…
- Choose the best statements that apply to…
- How would you present…

At the top of the hierarchical structure, we have evaluating and creating where students deepen thinking. Sentence stems such as:

Evaluating

- How could you verify…
- Can you evaluate the strategies used for…
- How does the use of data support your answer…
- Evaluate the function and impact of… when compared to…
- What are the possible outcomes of…
- What criteria would you use to…

Creating

- List the ways you can…
- How would you…
- Can you create an alternative pathway…

The learning cycle

- If the answer is... what could the question have been... are there alternatives...
- What would happen if...
- Is there a better solution...

Activity 3:
Ask a colleague to observe your lesson and focus on the questioning. Ask them to note down the following:

- The number of lower-order questions (a simple tally chart or total up from the who you asked method).
- The number of higher-order questions (a simple tally chart or total up from the who you asked method).
- Who you asked (use a simple seating plan and put a cross in green for a higher-order question directed to a student and a blue for a lower-order question).
- Do you use a 'no-hands-up' approach to keep students focused and ensure a good distribution.
- What your 'wait times' are.

Together sit and analyse the patterns and the distribution of the green and the blue crosses. Do you always ask those students who you know will get the answer correct the higher-order questions, thus limiting the higher-order development of other students? Do you ask mostly lower-order questions, if so how could this be developed to increase the number of higher-order questions?

The plenary

As we close our lesson, we need to allocate time to consolidate the learning. When we observe a lesson, this is often the phase that is rushed or worse still left out because of poor time management. The best teaching stops the lesson and makes time to consolidate the learning, whatever point your learners have reached.

For some lessons the Big Question will form your plenary session and will require extended thinking and development of the key points. For other lessons a different tool may be used to assess the learning.

Returning to the Big Question

When you return to the Big Question the power here is in the students identifying what they have learned in the lesson and in comparing their 'before' and 'after' response. How did they become more expert? What have they developed? What key knowledge did they need to improve their answer? This phase of course does not have to be done individually and there is great power in discussion in pairs. I would encourage you to apply the 'think, pair, share' technique at this phase and allow students time to think individually about their two responses, then discuss in pairs before you collectively discuss as a class. This is a very tangible activity where students can visibly see their learning.

Other activities

There are many activities that we can use in this phase, but the key is ensuring you are able to evaluate the learning of all students. This may mean you choose to use mini whiteboards so that you can visibly see the responses or if you ask for a written response you must take in the books and mark the response before the next lesson to ensure you have appropriately gauged the progress of the learners.

Other activities which make effective plenaries are:

- Identify the misconception and correcting a response
- Quiz ABCD questions
- Past exam questions requiring specific knowledge recall
- Making connections between images

Examples of activities are discussed in detail in Bartlett, 2015a, the important take-away here is that the plenary should allow the collective assessment of learning in your lesson based on the maximum of 4 knowledge points that you identified in the planning stage.

The classroom environment

This is an opportune moment to discuss the impact of the learning environment. There has been much work on sensory overload for students with learning needs such as autism or ADHD. We can control much of our learning environment,

The learning cycle

from the seating layout, the displays to the general tidiness. Ensuring that it is not a busy environment reduces extraneous load. This makes sense, doesn't it? If we go into a cluttered room with things randomly placed on tables, litter on the floor, broken blinds and very busy displays our brains may feel a little 'stressed' with the chaos. Contrast with a minimalistic room where displays are neatly organized, window ledges are clutter free, blinds are level, the desks are neat, ordered, and tidy. Immediately you 'feel different'. This is the same for our classrooms and we should aim to keep the rooms as calm as possible:

- Clear and simple displays
- Teacher desk clutter free
- Shelves neat and tidy with books well ordered
- Window ledge free of items
- Blinds level where possible
- Air circulating the room

Think yoga retreat – which focuses on relaxing the mind – how many do you see with clutter and busy colours? Next time you are in your classroom or conducting a learning walk around the academy focus on this and do a simple audit of your environment. Simple changes can make a big difference.

Activity 4:
In a CPD session create 2 classrooms (one untidy and the other well organized using the principles above) and ask staff in small groups or one by one to go into the room and write down their own thoughts about how they feel.

Displays also form an important part of our learning environment within the classroom, on corridors and in other spaces within the school. Displays are one of the first things that anyone coming into the school sees and it is that visual affirmation of our standards. Displays should be refreshed throughout the academic year, and they should be professional, visually aesthetic, and purposeful. Displays are a powerful communication tool for us and should be carefully thought out and always align with our school vision, values, and ethos.

We would strongly advise that you conduct a walk with a focus on your learning environment and key questions you should ask yourself include:

- Are the displays purposeful and professional or are they tired and of little relevance?

- Is the learning environment clean and tidy?
- Are books neatly aligned on the bookshelves and arranged in an orderly manner?
- Is the environment free of any damage or graffiti?
- Is the room well lit and well ventilated?
- Are corridor displays aligned with the school vision?
- Is every space in your school welcoming and exuding the school ethos?

Summary

In this chapter we have discussed the importance of cognitive load on learning and key features to consider when designing a lesson. Learning is different for every student and while there may be collective or common similarities there are always explicit or subtle differences. We must not lose sight that our perfectly planned lesson may not produce the learning we expected. If this happens it is important to deconstruct the lesson and usually with a peer or mentor and identify any hinge points.

An activity to support lesson development and review and to develop those critical questions is outlined below.

Activity 5:
Take a lesson from within your team. This may be a recently planned lesson or a previously planned shared resource. Complete a think, pair, share activity as a department identifying:

- Opportunities for the worked example effect
- The type of modelling and quality of the modelling phase
- Relevant information
- Any potential split attention effects – how might these be reduced or overcome?
- The modality effect – opportunities for both visual and auditory input
- How you implement the review phase

The learning cycle

- Opportunities for misconceptions
- Sensory input overload (presentation of the slides for example)

Checklist

- Have you taken the curriculum content and identified the powerful knowledge?
- Have you ensured learning is well sequenced?
- Have you identified the development of skills?
- Is cognitive load central to your planning?
- Have you maximized germane load, minimized extraneous load and managed intrinsic load?
- Is planning meticulous to account for dual coding?
- Have you carefully selected the Big Question based on the 4 most important knowledge points?
- Have you ensured a focus on literacy and used the Frayer model to decode?
- Does your learning cycle use the I do, we do, you do model to scaffold and support learning?
- Have you identified sensory input?
- Have you carefully considered the questions you will ask and the level of question along with possible misconceptions?
- Have you considered how you will 'know' learning has happened?
- Have you completed a walk with a focus on the learning environment?

Chapter 5

Assessing the curriculum

As students progress through the curriculum schemas become increasingly connected and complex. Effective assessment is necessary to identify knowledge gaps or misconceptions to ensure that students' knowledge is secure before allowing new connections to be made. Regular assessment should run parallel to curriculum progression and checks that teaching facilitates learning.

Assessment is the bridge between teaching and learning.

(William, 2011)

We commonly talk about two types of assessment in schools: formative assessment and summative assessment. In this chapter we focus on summative assessment which measures and evaluates students' knowledge and understanding of the intended curriculum and typically happens at the end of a unit of work.

The interim and end of composite assessment

The model of interim and end of composite assessment is a cycle of assessment used within a composite. The interim assessment takes place at the midpoint of the composite or as near to the midpoint as appropriate. It provides an opportunity to assess the quality of learning at a potential hinge point in the composite and allows any misconceptions or knowledge gaps to be identified. High-quality feedback should be provided to students and in a timely manner. This allows for early intervention to ensure students are then able to access the remainder of the composite. Figure 5.1 is an example of an interim assessment from a key stage 3 (KS3; ages 11 to 14) modern foreign language MFL composite (German): describing my family.

Assessing the curriculum

German Interim Assessment – Describing my family

Section 1: Reading

Read the paragraph below, then answer the following questions.

Ich heißen Sunita. I habe eine Mutter, einen Vater und zwei Brüder. Meine Eltern heißen Susan und John. Ich habe einen Hund, sie ist zehn Jahre alt. Ich liebe meinen Hund. Meine Brüder sind dreißig und einunddreißig Jahre alt. Meine Mutter und Vater wohnen in Bristol. Meine Brüder wohnen nicht bei meinen Eltern. Ich komme nicht gut mit Brüdern aus sie sind nervig und laut.

1. True or false? Circle the correct answer.
    a. Sunita has three brothers.   True / False
    b. Sunita's parents are called Susan and John.   True / False
    c. Sunita hates her dog.   True / False
    d. Sunita's family live in the same house.   True / False

2. How does Sunita describe her bothers?
   _____
   _____

Section 2: Writing

3. Translate the following sentence from German to English.
   Ich habe ein Schildkröte und zwölf Goldfische.
   _____
   _____

4. Translate the following sentence from English to German.
   I have two guinea pigs.
   _____
   _____

Figure 5.1 An example of an interim assessment taken from modern foreign languages (MFL)

Assessing the curriculum

An effective interim assessment:

- Uses concise and precise questions which elicit a specific response thus enabling the teacher to pinpoint which knowledge is secure, identify knowledge gaps and potential misconceptions.

- Only assesses the content that has been taught so far during the composite.

- Enables feedback to be provided that is specific and given in a timely manner.

Following the interim assessment, the curriculum should be adjusted to allow the remaining component knowledge to be taught.

The end of composite takes place at the end of the composite. The component knowledge is synthesized into a single assessment. Figure 5.2 is an example of an end of composite assessment from key stage 4 history.

The end of composite assessment should be carefully planned and assess as much of the taught component knowledge as possible. It is the knowledge we want students to commit to their long-term memory and it is the knowledge that would be re-activated when we revisit content. Questions should be specific and targeted. A question which is vague will not allow us to pinpoint misconceptions or knowledge gaps.

The length of composite is dependent on the amount of component knowledge and the inherent complexity. There is no one-size-fits-all approach, and it is important not to fall into the trap of a '6 week half term cycle'. In subjects such as mathematics and science the length of a composite is relatively short compared to a composite in art, for example, therefore it might not always be appropriate to complete an interim assessment and students would simply complete an end of composite assessment with regular formative assessment checks through the learning cycle.

"High crime rates in Whitechapel, at the end of the 19th Century, were a result of the Industrial Revolution".

To what extent do agree with this statement.

(15 marks)

Figure 5.2 An example of an end of composite assessment taken from key stage 4 history

Assessing the curriculum

Creating an assessment

The first step is to identify the key knowledge and construct a question which will allow you to 'test' that knowledge. Figure 5.3 is taken from a summary of the component knowledge from a key stage 4 science composite, alkenes and alkanes.

The type of assessment is also important. Traditionally assessments have fallen into two categories: written and practical. For example, in physical education assessment is typically practical, whereas in science it is written. The most appropriate form of assessment is determined by the curriculum knowledge itself. In Chapter 3 we identified the different types of curriculum knowledge: substantive, disciplinary, procedural, and declarative. Ensure assessment is of the core knowledge and not hinterland knowledge.

It is a common misconception that procedural knowledge ('students will know how to …') is only assessed through practical means. In food technology where

---

Summary of component knowledge: What are alkanes and alkenes?

- Students will know that alkanes and alkenes are hydrocarbons. A hydrocarbon only contains hydrogen and carbon.
- Students will be able to name alkanes and alkenes with up to 5 carbon atoms.
- Students will know that the bonding in alkanes and alkenes are covalent bonds.
- Students will know the general molecular formula for alkanes is C_nH_{2n+2}. Students will be able to use this formula to identify the number of carbon atoms when given the number of hydrogen atoms and vice versa.
- Students will know that in an alkane the bond between hydrogen and carbon are single.
- Students will know how to draw the structure of an alkane.
- Students will know the general molecular formula for alkenes is C_nH_{2n}. Students will be able to use this formula to identify the number of carbon atoms when given the number of hydrogen atoms and vice versa.
- Students will know that in an alkene there is one double bond and the rest are single bond between hydrogen and carbon atoms.
- Students will know how to draw the structure of an alkene.
- Students will know that bromine water can test the presence of an alkene. The solution will change from orange/brown to colourless.

Figure 5.3 An example taken from science illustrating a summary of component knowledge

the students are developing their procedural knowledge of how to use different cutting techniques to cut vegetables, it will be more appropriate for the students to demonstrate these cutting techniques practically. Whereas in statistics where students have been studying how to carry out different sampling techniques, this might prove difficult if you wish to demonstrate this physically by sampling a large group of people. It might be more appropriate for them to compare different sampling methods and evaluate which is the most appropriate.

All subjects have declarative knowledge 'students will know that ...'. For example, in physical education students' knowledge of the rules of netball could be assessed by showing the students a series of video clips from a netball game and asking students to comment on the rules of the game. This can be done orally or in written form and provides an opportunity to assess the acquisition of disciplinary literacy.

For all subjects, substantive and disciplinary knowledge should be assessed. For example, in science you might want to assess the knowledge of scientific investigation, this can be done through the lens of substantive knowledge. The students will be required to form a hypothesis, plan the investigation, test the hypothesis, analyse the results and form a conclusion. This assessment might take place over a series of lessons where feedback might be provided at each stage. The converse is also true, for example in religious studies you can integrate assessment of students' substantive and disciplinary knowledge by asking them to use sources of authority in their arguments or in history compare and contrast two sources.

Selecting the right questions

The assessment is designed to evaluate the students' progression through the curriculum. Selecting the right questions that will enable you to pinpoint the knowledge gaps is critical.

Multiple choice questions, when designed well, can be used as a diagnostic tool to identify particular misconceptions. These might be particularly useful when designing the interim assessment. Figure 5.4 is an example of a multiple-choice question.

Key features of a well-designed multiple-choice question:

- The answer is not obvious; therefore, students are not able to use the process of elimination to guess the answer.

- The incorrect options reveal a specific misconception linked to the component knowledge.

Assessing the curriculum

Terry buys a coat for £51 in the sale.

The price of the coat was discounted by 15%

How much was the coat before the sale?

Tick (✓) the correct answer.

£58.65 ☐   £60 ☐   £43.35 ☐   £66 ☐

Figure 5.4 Example of a multiple-choice question from KS3 mathematics

Questions which require an extended response assess chains of component knowledge. Below is a GCSE-style science question.

Compare alkenes with alkanes.

In your answer you should refer to:

- The chemical structure of alkanes and alkenes
- Combustion of alkanes and alkenes
- How to test for the presence of an alkene in a mixture

(10 marks)

When designing questions that require an extended response, it is important that you support students to form the chains of component knowledge and guide their thinking. If the question above had just been 'compare alkenes with alkanes', the students' responses to the question will vary in quality as the question is too open. There is a time and a place for open questions which provide a challenge to students, however, if the purpose is to assess the composite knowledge, then this might not be the most appropriate.

When designing an assessment, you might be using assessment questions from a variety of sources; those perhaps designed in-house or from an external source, such as an exam bank. Whatever the source of the question it is important to ensure it facilities a specific response based on the component knowledge. Figure 5.5 illustrates the summary knowledge from a KS3 computer science composite titled 'how does a computer process data?'

Assessing the curriculum

> **Summary of component knowledge: How does a computer process data?**
>
> - Students will know that a binary digit is often referenced as a bit. A bit is represented by either a 1 or a 0
> - Students will know that denary numbers are numbers written in base 10, for example 345.
> - Students will know how to convert denary numbers to binary (up to 8-bit).
> - Students will know how to convert binary numbers (up to 8-bit) to denary.
> - Students will know how to add and subtract numbers written in binary (up to 8-bit), where the result does not lead to overflow.

Figure 5.5 An illustration of the summary knowledge in a computer science composite

Here is a sample of the questions taken from the end of composite assessment.

Question 1: Convert 10111 from binary to denary form.

Question 2: Convert 300 to binary.

Question 3: Add the following numbers written in binary 10111 and 1111101.

On the surface all the questions appear to be suitable for the assessment. However, question 2 and question 3 fall outside the remit of the component knowledge within this composite. The answer for question 2 is 100101100 which is 9 bits in length. The component knowledge only requires the student to convert to binary numbers up to 8 bits in length. The answer for question 3 requires the students to have an understanding on overflow which is not explicitly taught in the curriculum. While it may sound obvious, it is therefore essential to ensure the question links to the component.

Scaffolding assessment

Inclusion for all students is a fundamental element of curriculum development, and we must therefore consider how assessment is inclusive for all students; scaffolding is commonly used. Let us consider the type of question which requires an extended response (typically the 4 or above mark questions in examinations). The 8-mark question below is an example taken from a GCSE-style business studies examination question and requires students to make a recommendation and to justify their decision.

Assessing the curriculum

Example 1:
Olivia owns a cake shop. She is launching a new range of healthier cupcake options to attract new customers to her cake shop. She is considering an advertising campaign using either social media or local radio.

> Recommend which method Olivia should use. Justify your answer.
>
> (8 marks)

To achieve maximum number of marks the response requires a comparison of two methods, along with justification. Unfortunately, many students simply wrote the single method they would choose; this is because to answer the question they need to be able to understand how to structure a response and what each command word requires. Herein lies the problem, the examination question assesses not necessarily their knowledge but their ability to interpret and independently scaffold their answer. When we asked a group of students to complete this question direct followed by the scaffolded version, 93% of students achieved 6 or more marks on the scaffolded question when compared to 40% on the original question without an intervention (students were asked to first attempt the un-scaffolded question followed immediately by the scaffolded question). We could argue here that capital (discussed in Chapter 6) comes into play; we know capital impacts on outcomes. We then enter the minefield of parity and fairness in examination systems and whether we are assessing the skill to interpret or the subject content knowledge. Of course, both are important in determining a student's proficiency in a subject, but we should ask ourselves if the weighting is sensible and if the balance ensures we do not disadvantage the disadvantaged. Most importantly we need to ensure that our students are equipped with the skillset to answer an un-scaffolded question and there are many techniques that you will be aware of, for example, PEEL and PEARL. Our role is to support the gradual removal of scaffolding. The same question is scaffolded in the example below:

Example 2:
Olivia owns a cake shop. She is launching a new range of healthier cupcake options to attract new customers to her cake shop. She is considering an advertising campaign using either social media or local radio.
Recommend which method Olivia should use. Justify your answer.

> Paragraph 1: State one advantage and one disadvantage of using social media.
> Paragraph 2: State one advantage and one disadvantage of using local radio.

Paragraph 3: State which method would be most appropriate for this business (ensure you consider the context of the business).

(8 marks)

To achieve the 8 marks the student would need to know and recall the specific knowledge but does so through a framework.

Feedback

Providing high-quality feedback to students improves learning. Effective student feedback has an effect size of +0.6 on student progress (EEF, 2021b). Gathering feedback on how well students have learned a topic is important in enabling teachers to address any misunderstanding and provide the right level of challenge in future lessons.

How effective a particular type of feedback is depends on many factors, including the ability of the learner, how motivated the learner is, the type of task being undertaken, and the learning goals set. We should not regard feedback as a 'silver bullet'. For feedback to be impactful, other components of high-quality teaching and learning are needed, such as, considered planning and clear goal setting and the opportunity for further practice. Feedback has limited impact if there is no meaningful opportunity for the student to use it either directly or in an applied context.

Question level analysis

Following an assessment, it is not uncommon for data to be synthesized at question level analysis (QLA). This is particularly useful if you have multiple questions that link to the component knowledge from the curriculum as it provides an immediate horizontal (individual student) and vertical (whole class overview) visual. Figure 5.6 is an example of a question level analysis spreadsheet.

Immediately we are able to see that questions 6 and 11 have not been answered well and this may be because the curriculum is poor in this area and needs to be reviewed or the question was not specific to the component knowledge or the quality of teaching was poor. If when the data is amalgamated at year level there is a particular class that has 'red or amber' for a given question when compared to all other students, then it is likely this is linked to the quality of teaching and this can be addressed through coaching. However, if the whole year group is

Assessing the curriculum

End of Composite Assessment	Question 1	Question 2	Question 3	Question 4	Question 5	Question 6	Question 7	Question 8	Question 9	Question 10	Question 11	Question 12	Total
Maximum Number of Marks	1	1	6	4	2	1	2	2	12	2	2	6	41
Student A	1	1	6	3	2	1	2	2	5	1	0	4	28
Student B	1	1	5	4	2	0	1	2	3	2	0	5	26
Student C	1	1	5	4	2	0	1	2	4	2	0	5	27
Student D	0	1	3	0	2	0	1	2	5	2	0	4	20
Student E	1	1	6	1	2	0	1	2	5	1	0	5	25
Student F	0	0	0	0	1	0	2	2	3	0	0	6	14
Student G	1	0	1	3	2	0	2	2	2	2	1	6	22
Student H	1	1	4	3	2	0	0	2	1	2	0	6	22
Student I	1	1	4	2	0	0	0	2	4	2	0	6	22
Student J	0	1	4	4	0	1	1	2	2	2	0	6	23
Average	0.7	0.8	3.8	2.4	1.5	0.2	1.1	2	3.4	1.6	0.1	5.3	23

Figure 5.6 Class question level analysis where green is secure, amber is some curriculum awareness and knowledge and red is no curriculum knowledge

'amber/red' for a given question it may suggest either the question was not specific or the quality of the curriculum needs to be reviewed in this area. There are lots of interesting exercises that can be done at QLA including:

- Teacher group analysis
- Whole year group analysis
- SEND analysis
- Disadvantaged student analysis

All of which should be considered in the context of curriculum review. For example, is our curriculum fully accessible for all students? Does our curriculum team require further professional development in a given area?

When we look at question level analysis horizontally, we are looking at an individual student's results and this is where we can build bespoke intervention. This level of analysis should be done by all class teachers and then discussed with the Head of Department following each assessment. If we continue to 'plough through' the curriculum without addressing an individual student's knowledge gaps then there was little purpose to the assessment in the first place as those gaps will continue to widen.

All school leaders understand the importance of providing meaningful feedback; do all teachers? Done well, feedback supports student progress, builds

Assessing the curriculum

End of Composite Assessment		Marks		Total
Curriculum Knowledge	Component Knowledge 1	0 / 5	Results	**18**
	Component Knowledge 2	4 / 4		
	Component Knowledge 3	5 / 6		Curriculum Score
	Component Knowledge 4	1 / 3		3
	Component Knowledge 5	2 / 3		Effort
	Component Knowledge 6	6 / 12		1

Figure 5.7 An example of an end of composite student level QLA

learning, addresses misunderstandings, and thereby closes the gap between a student's present knowledge status and where the teacher wants them to be. Much consideration has also been given to the methods by which feedback is delivered. Should feedback be written, or should it be verbal?

A useful feedback tool for students is a summary of the QLA by component knowledge (and for example component knowledge may be assessed through 2 or 3 questions). This highlights for students the areas they are secure in or the areas that require further support. An example is shown in Figure 5.7.

When the assessment is an extended written response, producing a question level analysis is not the most the appropriate feedback method. Figure 5.8 is an example of an extended written response from science. Here you can see that the teacher has highlighted the correct knowledge in green and the incorrect knowledge in pink.

We should note here that caution should be taken if a student's response is majority 'pink' as feedback will be a negative student experience and therefore a discussion between the class teacher and student is a more balanced approach. Highlighting alone also does nothing more than indicate 'correct' or 'incorrect' statements and teacher feedback to extended responses needs to provide more detail as illustrated in Figure 5.9. A common approach is the 'what went well, WWW' and the 'even better if, EBI'.

Re-teach

When students complete an assessment, our next step is to review the assessments and schools often have a policy of 're-teach'. Put simply this means teaching the topics where students scored poorly again. Where re-teach is carefully considered and done well it has an impact on the learner and where it is done

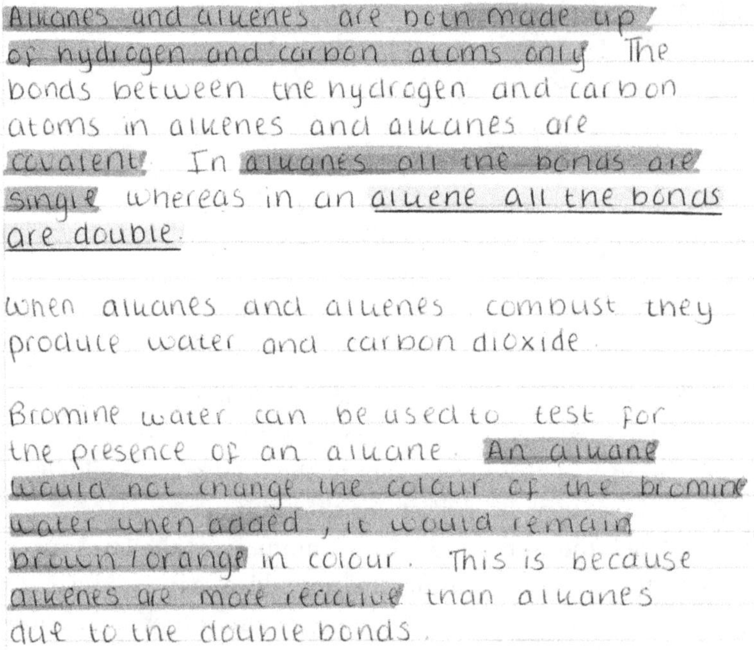

Assessing the curriculum

> Alkanes and alkenes are both made up of hydrogen and carbon atoms only. The bonds between the hydrogen and carbon atoms in alkenes and alkanes are covalent. In alkanes all the bonds are single whereas in an alkene all the bonds are double.
>
> When alkanes and alkenes combust they produce water and carbon dioxide.
>
> Bromine water can be used to test for the presence of an alkane. An alkane would not change the colour of the bromine water when added, it would remain brown/orange in colour. This is because alkenes are more reactive than alkanes due to the double bonds.

Figure 5.8 An extended written piece in science where highlighting provides immediate visual feedback

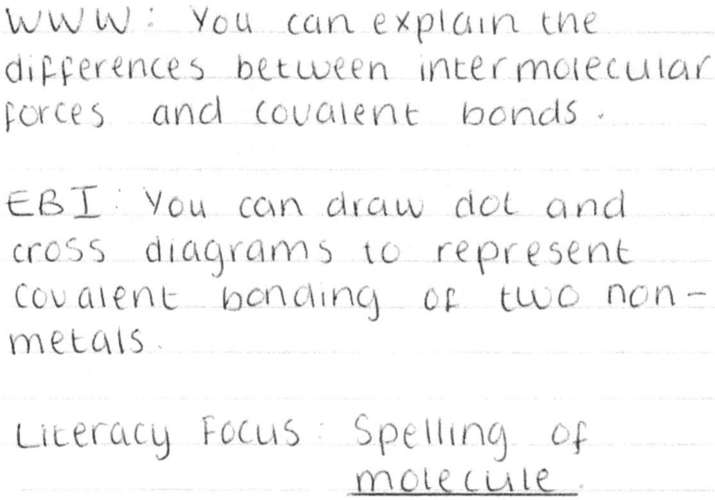

> WWW: You can explain the differences between intermolecular forces and covalent bonds.
>
> EBI: You can draw dot and cross diagrams to represent covalent bonding of two non-metals.
>
> Literacy Focus: Spelling of molecule.

Figure 5.9 An example of WWW and EBI feedback approach in science

poorly it is simply a wasted session. Unfortunately, because little professional development time is invested in sharing best practice for re-teach, it means many teachers simply deliver 'more of the same'. By this we mean they teach the same lesson again or they make minor tweaks but are ultimately teaching the same lesson. This is obviously based on the premise that if we deliver the same content again suddenly the student will understand it. However, simply teaching the same lesson is a crude approach as it may reinforce misconceptions or create greater confusion for the learner.

The very best approach to re-teach is to begin with the curriculum. Unpick students' responses to the question in the assessment; was it the curriculum knowledge that is insecure or was it the question? This is where a question level analysis is a useful tool for identifying which questions the students performed poorly on.

If it is the question, then you need to identify if there is an unusual word that the students did not understand or whether it was a lack of exam technique. For example, statistics GCSE questions require good comprehension skills. Students with lower reading ages will find this more challenging and yet if it was scaffolded would most likely be able to apply the mathematical process. Knowing that this is the style of examination we must ensure that we prepare our students in the best possible way and that comprehension becomes part of our statistics curriculum. This is not simply giving children 'wordy' questions or more of the same. It is about equipping students with the skills to decode a question. Figure 5.10 is an example of a question whereby the students are required to determine the most appropriate mathematical method without the method being explicitly referred to in the question. In this case lowest common multiples.

This naturally differs from a question which explicitly identifies the process such as

- Factorize $x^2 + 5x + 6$

- Expand and simplify $(x + 4)(x - 2)$

Questions that involve higher levels of comprehension, such as Figure 5.10, increase the need to decode. If students cannot decode with automaticity, then the cognitive load becomes too high and gaps in the learning process may form. If the question had been explicit, such as, 'work out the lowest common multiple of 15, 20, and 3', it is more likely the students would be able to respond accurately as this involves direct recall of a mathematical process and then

Assessing the curriculum

> Derek is organising a birthday party. He is going to give the guests party favours. He decides in to give each guest a balloon, a lollipop and a small toy.
>
> Balloons are sold in packets of 15
>
> Lollipops are sold in packets of 20
>
> Small toys are sold in packets of 3
>
> Derek wants to buy the same number of balloons, lollipops and small toys.
>
> Work out the smallest number of packets of each item he should buy.
>
> _____ packets of balloons
>
> _____ packets of lollipops
>
> _____ packets of small toys
>
> (3 marks)

Figure 5.10 An example of a word problem in mathematics without explicit reference to the mathematical process (lowest common multiple)

applying it to three numbers. It does not involve students needing to select the most appropriate method.

Similarly in English examination questions a simple word that a student may not understand, or an unusual vocabulary choice in a question, can create extraneous load and prevent a student from accessing their schema of knowledge about a particular text, potentially leading to an inaccuracy in response. We discuss the impact of capital on student outcomes in Chapter 6.

For a question which requires comprehension, the first stage of re-teach would be to decode the question. Modelling how to approach the question is a useful tool here; a 'thinking aloud approach'.

The question shown in Figure 5.10 can be decoded to support students in identifying the most appropriate mathematical process. As you read the question you should train the students to highlight any key phrases and/or points of relevant information. In this question 'buy the same number' and 'smallest number' would be highlighted. The word 'same' is a synonym for 'common'. Therefore, students should be able to identify they are being asked to work out a 'common' number of balloons, lollipops, and toys. The word 'smallest' is a synonym for

Assessing the curriculum

'lowest'. Linking the two together should suggest to the student they need to find the lowest common number or lowest common multiple of 15, 20, and 3. Training the students to identify key phrases from the text and apply their understanding of key terminology will support them in selecting the appropriate mathematical process. Once the process of answering the question is modelled to the students, we can apply the 'I do, we do, you do' model discussed in Chapter 4 and provide the students with a similar problem to solve.

Of course, a poor response can be because the student either has a lack of curriculum knowledge or a misconception or a lack of motivation. By knowing your students and looking forensically at each student's response, you can identify individual needs but also more generally accumulate any common approaches to the question and/or common errors. Figure 5.11 shows two incorrect responses to the same dividing fraction question.

These responses are both incorrect and both 'scored' the same mark. If we simply went by a score on the QLA spreadsheet we would not be addressing the root cause. Student A and Student B have different curriculum knowledge gaps. Student A is unable to convert a mixed number fraction to an improper fraction, yet they demonstrated understanding of the process of dividing fractions. Intervention here would focus on converting mixed number fractions. Student B can convert mixed number fractions to improper fractions, however, their understanding of dividing fractions is poor. Student B's feedback would focus on the process of dividing fractions. This raises the debate about the purpose of the questions we use: is it to pinpoint a specific skill or is it to determine if students can combine skills? If we are using a question which combines two or more methods or processes, we should consider how we use the QLA. Better

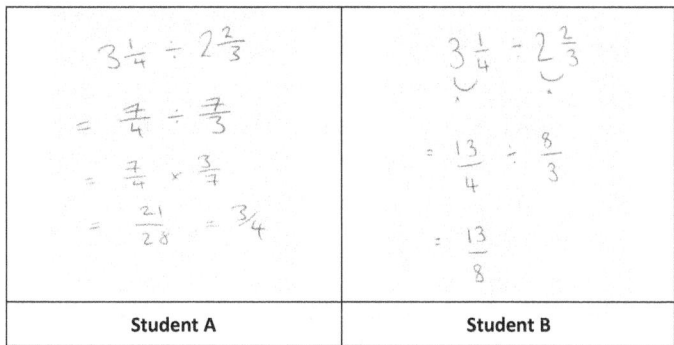

Figure 5.11 An example of two student responses to the same question

Assessing the curriculum

at the interim or end of composite stage would be to have questions which, for example, convert a mixed number to an improper fraction and questions which only have the skill of dividing fractions. This would then allow us to pinpoint any gaps. However, this draws us to the discussion about the purpose of the assessment and there is an argument for both approaches as learners move to mastering the questions naturally becomes more complicated and will most likely involve two or more concepts or processes.

When we plan for re-teach, we should therefore consider some key points:

- Review the question and identify where extraneous load was created.

- Look at the sequencing within our curriculum and identify opportunities where knowledge gaps might have occurred.

- Consider how we taught and sequenced the knowledge in the first place
    - were misconceptions created through poor modelling
    - how effectively does the curriculum support de-coding

One of the dangers of re-teach currently is that some teachers simply deliver more of the same and this is counterproductive and can reinforce misconceptions. Unpick the question and then review the lesson itself. Identify the key features of that specific question and begin to decode the challenges that students faced. If it was a knowledge gap, then this is straightforward, and the curriculum review should ensure that this knowledge is inserted into a component. If, however, it involved, for example, the inability to comprehend or decode a question, then this involves a much deeper re-teach and a consideration of how we deliver our curriculum or how we develop conceptual understanding.

Re-testing in the case of a knowledge gap has impact much the same way as knowledge retrieval (discussed in Chapter 4). Essentially teach the required knowledge and re-test. This then supports long-term memory and learning. We must of course examine what we are testing. For example, teaching a student some key points of knowledge, then testing them immediately and again at a spaced point tests how well they have learned or retained specific facts. Transfer testing, however, is considered more powerful and is where we teach students and then we ask them to apply it to a similar but different scenario. This tests how well students understand the underlying concepts rather than how well they remember a list of facts and is known as transfer testing. We can still test the immediate and delayed retention but we are testing understanding and not the ability to recall a list of facts. If we are re-testing transfer then we must look closely at how we re-teach conceptual knowledge.

Re-testing in the case of the decoding is more complicated and, without a re-teach that challenges the underlying concept, this is a deeper challenge. In fact, this most likely involves a more dynamic re-think on curriculum implementation. Re-testing more of the same in this case may have a negative impact if applied in the same way as a knowledge gap re-test and will only be successful when students have the necessary decoding skills.

When planning assessments aim to support germane cognitive load and alongside this we must have an acute awareness of any extraneous load which potentially disadvantages already disadvantaged students further, creating an educational 'gap'. Our goal is to be a keen critical eye on our curriculum and to ensure our learning conversations within our subject teams and with senior leaders produce the best possible environment to support student outcomes.

Summary

Without effective assessment, implementation and curriculum development will be limited. Effective assessment supports the individual learner and contributes to the cycle of curriculum improvement. In this chapter we explored the importance of the type of assessment and challenged the purpose of our assessments.

Checklist

- Are your assessments carefully mapped and aligned to the curriculum?
- What form of assessment is most appropriate for the curriculum knowledge?
- How are you assessing both substantive and disciplinary knowledge?
- Have you checked the suitability of the questions to ensure you are getting the right information from the students?
- How are you going to provide feedback?
- Through what medium will you deliver feedback?
- How are you going to integrate re-testing into the curriculum?
- How are you going to review the relevant composite and any linked curriculum based on the triangulation of assessment data, student and staff voice, student workbook reviews, and implementation reviews?

Assessing the curriculum

An effective curriculum review of the medium-term plan may include:

- Compliance checks on whether there is evidence that all the component knowledge was covered in the curriculum.
- What specific misconceptions the students had during the teaching of the component, identified through assessment, student and staff voice and student workbooks.
- The effectiveness and impact of scaffolding.
- How well students' knowledge of disciplinary knowledge is being developed across the curriculum.
- Any variation in student indicators such as SEND or disadvantaged students.

Chapter 6

Social, cultural, and educational capital

The curriculum as a learning tool is more than simply 'what students will know'. Intrinsically the curriculum develops educational capital but there is the opportunity to provide a much richer and deeper learning experience through the inclusion of social and cultural capital. When all three forms of capital combine, we create a powerful learning experience for our students. In this chapter we begin to explore what we mean by each form of capital.

Capital, by definition, is a broad term for anything that gives someone value or advantage. Our role is to 'open doors' for our students and we use the curriculum as a vehicle to develop skills and knowledge. Whether explicitly or subconsciously we create social, cultural, and educational capital. The differential between schools becomes their awareness of the fundamental principles of capital gain.

Many schools separate 'cultural capital' and isolate it to a curriculum of personal development through SMSC or PHSE, seeing cultural capital as an 'add on'. Of course, this is fool's gold because to successfully enrich students' education and to 'level the playing field' for our disadvantaged students we must embed cultural and social capital within our subject curriculums alongside the wider school values and ethos. Cultural and social capital needs to be built into the foundations of our practice.

Cultural capital

Cultural capital was introduced in the 1970s by Pierre Bourdieu, a French sociologist. Bourdieu refers to the impact of cultural and social knowledge on the progress students can make. He defines cultural capital as having three sources: objective, embodied, and institutionalized.

Social, cultural, and educational capital

- Objective: cultural possessions such as literature, pieces of art, cultural artefacts

- Embodied: mannerisms, gestures, posture, language, preferences

- Institutionalized: qualifications, academic credentials

There is much research on the comparative educational outcomes of disadvantaged students and non-disadvantaged students. Cultural and social capital gained through the 'family' environment supports all students to do better in school and there is considerable research that looks at the impact of social and cultural capital on educational outcomes. Those students who, for example, are encouraged to read and discuss a variety of texts at home, have taken music lessons or are encouraged to appreciate a wide range of music, who have visited museums, theatres and art galleries or indeed other countries and those who have an awareness of heritage, are able to contextualize knowledge or utilize the skills they develop to enhance their learning experience when in school and they have a much greater awareness of where that learning sits in the 'big picture'. They can make connections more easily and they are able to develop their network of schema. Those students who do not gain such experiences in their family environment are disadvantaged in capital to their peers.

An important point is that this is not about a family's level of income; to read a book costs nothing (go to a library) and similarly many museums and art galleries have free entry. This is about families taking the time and spending time interested and engaging in learning with their children. Yet while we state that this is not income related, we know that there is a gap between outcomes for disadvantaged and non-disadvantaged students and the definition of disadvantaged is associated with household income; the great quandary of educational inequality. We further note that the lower levels of reading are associated with socioeconomic status and so there is a potential causal effect and cycle we must break.

The work done by John Hattie *(Hattie effect size list – 256 Influences Related To Achievement <www.visible-learning.org>)* was discussed in Chapter 4 and the effect sizes of note here are:

- Parental involvement +0.50

- Positive family dynamics +0.52

- Socio economic status +0.52

Phrases such as 'levelling up' are commonly used, with the aim that schools ensure that background and in particular disadvantage plays less of a role in educational success and social mobility. Much has and continues to be invested in this area and we should acknowledge that a gap still exists. In this chapter we encourage you to look closely at your curriculum and ensure that at our fundamental core we don't unintentionally disadvantage the disadvantaged. Cultural capital is an opportunity to bring learning to life.

Literacy and cultural capital

Cultural capital is intrinsically linked to language, vocabulary, and the development of schema. Literacy levels impact on educational outcomes and both social and cultural development. The National Literacy Trust refers to the cycle of social mobility and challenges the fairness in society, with the impact of poor literacy skills being intergenerational 'holds a person back at every stage of their life. As a child they won't be able to succeed at school, as a young adult they will be locked out of the job market, and as a parent they won't be able to support their own child's learning' (https://literacytrust.org.uk).

The National Literacy Trust research shows that 383,755 children and young people in the United Kingdom don't have a book of their own and disadvantaged children are more likely than their peers to not own a book (9.3% versus 6%). Being below the functional reading age of 11 impacts on health, financial prospects, mental health, and life expectancy. Incredibly, '16.4% of adults in England, or 7.1 million people, can be described as having 'very poor literacy skills'. Adults with poor literacy skills will be locked out of the job market and, as a parent, they won't be able to support their child's learning' (National Literacy Trust, <https://literacytrust.org.uk/parents-and-families/adult-literacy/>). Put simply 1 in 6 adults in England have literacy difficulties. The statistics for poor literacy skills from the National Literacy Trust are stark and are summarized below (please note, however, that each nation has its own definition of basic literacy skills and so direct comparisons cannot be made):

- England: 1 in 6 (16.4%)
- Wales: 1 in 8 (12%)
- Scotland: 1 in 4 (26.7%)
- Northern Ireland: 1 in 5 (17.9%)

Social, cultural, and educational capital

Developing literacy needs to be at the heart of our curriculum and this can be done in many ways. Having high expectations of how we model literacy and language as teachers and how we promote and develop oracy should be central to our curriculum.

Let us consider what we mean by reading. Reading is an interpretive and interactive skill which involves decoding alongside an active cognitive thinking process. It is our ability to interpret from a written page (of lots of letters) meaning and information. Reading comprehension strategies which develop a student's understanding of written text have a high impact on a student's development of language and curricular literacy. Reading comprehension involves students using linguistic knowledge and schema to create contextual understanding. When students comprehend a text, they are able to 'create a mental representation of a typical instance which helps people to make sense of a word more quickly because people assimilate new experiences by activating the schema in their minds' (Cook, 1997). To learn from what we read we link information to what is already in our memory. In order to allow students to learn we must create an environment which allows students to concentrate and ensure our curriculum deepens learning through the cultural and social capital we develop.

There are many strategies used to support comprehension and reciprocal reading is an example of a reading comprehension strategy which involves a dialogue between the teacher and student to construct the meaning of text. The dialogue includes four basic components: predicting, questioning, clarifying, and summarizing. This helps students to become more metacognitive about their reading and learning supporting them to become more active, reflective, and strategic readers. When students learn the techniques and each role has been modelled by the teacher, they become the teacher themselves in a small group setting leading a dialogue about what they have read. Each role has a different purpose:

- The Predictor: to offer predictions about what might happen next in the text.

- The Questioner: to ask questions about unclear parts of the text and to explore connections to other concepts they have already learned.

- The Clarifier: to answer the questions posed by the Questioner and to provide additional clarification and examples.

- The Summarizer: to summarize key information and ideas generated from the text.

The teacher acts as a guide and supports the process. This can be used at any level and for any type of material, from fiction to academic research texts. It develops a student's ability to build on knowledge and to further develop their schema. It is important that students are able to make decisions on their own about how to make sense of a text (Gambrell and Morrow, 2015). Reciprocal reading teaches these strategies for students to develop their own thinking when they read. Our ultimate goal is to develop reader fluency 'freedom from word identification problems that might hinder comprehension' (Harris and Hodges, 1995). Fluency includes comprehension.

Vocabulary tiers help teaching as we can organize words effectively to support learning. Students must be able to process tier 2 and 3 vocabulary if they are to comprehend higher-level subject texts. There are three tiers of vocabulary:

- Tier 1: high frequency, everyday words that do not typically require explicit teaching. Examples include table, house, go, eat.

- Tier 2: ambitious words that learners are exposed to across a range of subjects and in different contexts more familiar to mature language users. Examples include analyse, context, emerge, comprehend, reaction.

- Tier 3: subject-specific words such as numerator, photosynthesis, radiation. This is vocabulary specifically required to teach content knowledge.

The Frayer model, developed by Dorothy Frayer in 1969, is a model used to support the development of literacy decoding. The model offers students a visual representation where they define the word, identify key facts or characteristics, provide examples and non-examples. This may also extend to an image. Students are prompted to develop their comprehension, understanding words in a wider context. It also supports students to make connections and to activate prior learning developing their schema and can be used effectively to support tier 2 and 3 vocabulary.

You can use the Frayer model in lots of different ways, for example, complete each of the four boxes but leave the central word missing. Students must utilize their skills to identify the missing word. Equally you could leave one of the four outer boxes blank. Figure 6.1 illustrates the Frayer model, decoding 'perimeter'.

Knowledge and cultural capital

We discussed in earlier chapters the importance of identifying the 'essential' or 'powerful' knowledge for each composite and the standard reference points that

Social, cultural, and educational capital

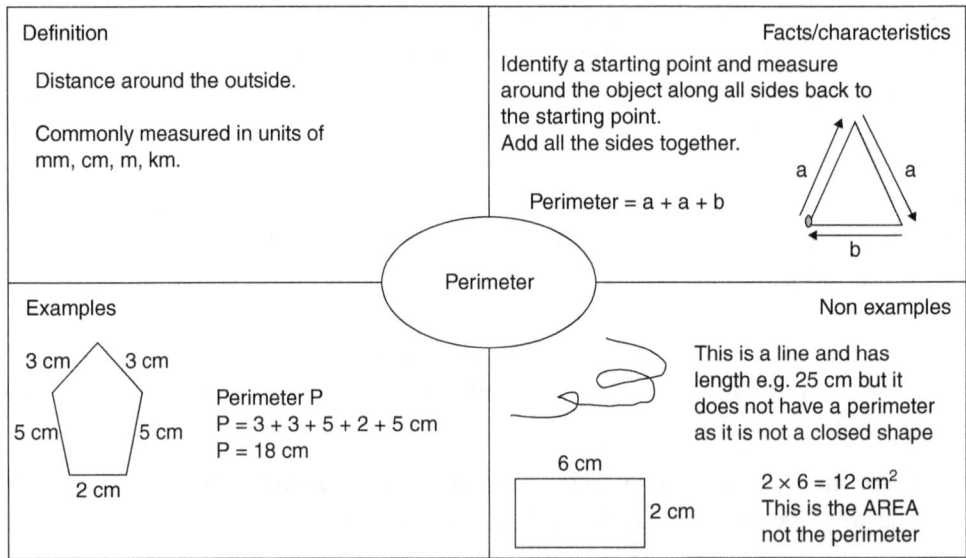

Figure 6.1 An example of the Frayer model for the word 'Perimeter'

form the basis of the developing schema. It is the connections that we support our students to make and the formation of strong schema that begin to address the cultural capital gap. If our curriculum consists of a series of learned knowledge points, then enhanced learning may not happen or may not happen well and learning becomes low level which limits the contextual development and simply becomes an exercise in how well a student can memorize a list of facts.

When we develop knowledge, we must always look at our starting point and this is not simply 'what do students already know'. This is about the capital they already have. Let us consider that in an English lesson we are asking our students to write a poem about the seaside. If our students have never been to the seaside, then how are they able to write a poem about it? They have no capital. They may know what the sea is and what the sand is (by definition) but fundamentally if they have never experienced the seaside, they are deficient in capital. We know funding constraints mean we cannot simply take all our students to the seaside to provide the experiential learning and so we must therefore begin to think outside of the box. In this case, how can we bring the seaside to the classroom? How can we capture those concepts? We need to address this before we even get to writing a poem or creative piece. Pause and reflect at this moment about how you might do this. I am sure you have come up with many different ideas, images, videos, Google Earth, looking at the sights and sounds, a sandbox for

Social, cultural, and educational capital

them to walk in to feel the sand beneath their feet, promoting the vocabulary we may use and generating a wall of words. If you are fortunate to have a virtual classroom as many future builds do, you may even be able to generate the smells and students can get the 4D experience.

Now, reflect for a moment, if we were asking students instead to write a creative writing piece about the Amazon rainforest, most likely we would already have factored in a need to develop prior knowledge before commencing any activity and we would have spent considerable time planning how we build this learning. You would probably have developed this over a lesson or series of lessons. In contrast, with the seaside example, there is a danger that we make an assumption, an assumption about a prior experience or knowledge base, because we may think (or hope) that going to the seaside is part of everyone's childhood experience. Just because a piece of the curriculum is about something that is more tangible to us, or we imagine more tangible to others does not mean that it is, and we need to apply the same process to all areas of our curriculum. I add a caveat here and that is time because as we all know curriculum time is precious in education and for this reason looking at the curriculum as a whole and not as isolated composites or components is critical as we begin to make the connections and identify opportunities for the development of schema. Equally ploughing ahead and 'squeezing' something into a preconceived period can mean that we de-value the potential learning experience.

Activity 1:
CPD opportunity: An interesting exercise for a CPD session to emphasize this to colleagues is to pick something rather random and ask them to write a poem about it. For example, you may pick the 'life of the Elephant shrew' – most likely they will know nothing about this and staff will experience the uncomfortable position that many of our students find themselves in on a daily basis: they can make no connections with prior knowledge, there are no schema – they can't access the far-reaching parts of their brain where there may be some knowledge to connect to. Provide staff with a piece of research, watch a small clip, look at images and habitat – now ask them to do the same. You will see pens start to write! It is the feeling you want staff to capture, this isn't really about the exercise itself.

There are so many examples of the above where we may wonder as teachers why we see some blank faces, or we wonder why a student hasn't completed something to the expected level. We must remember that many children will not want to admit in front of peers that they have not, for example, been to the

Social, cultural, and educational capital

seaside or been to a museum. My plea here, and you will note I keep repeating this phrase, is to ensure we don't inadvertently disadvantage the disadvantaged, to think about each stage of your curriculum and how you can bring this to life. Our vantage point in this arena is technology. If you're talking about an art gallery, take them on a virtual tour. If you're going to Australia, Google Earth the location. If you're studying India in geography, talk to the food technology team – can their dishes for part of that period focus on cultural food? If you are studying a play, then can you bring the theatre to school by using for example the free resource from the National Theatre which broadcasts plays to schools (<www.nationaltheatre.org.uk/learning/national-theatre-collection/uk-state-funded-schools>) or could you look to fund a local theatre company to come into school for a live performance.

With OFSTED highlighting cultural capital in the 2019 framework, we saw a flurry of schools highlighting things in their curriculum and where this was done poorly it was simply an 'add on' which most likely caused confusion and had little to no impact on learning. The fundamental principle here is that we need to invest properly in the professional development of our teams.

Where cultural capital is intertwined in the curriculum it becomes a powerful tool to transform learning. Much of this comes down in the early stages to staff training and development and ultimately making this an embedded part of the culture of the school. I've never met a teacher who wants to do something badly but the key to ensuring things are done well is equipping people with the skills and understanding to do it. OFSTED describe cultural capital as 'the essential knowledge that pupils need to be educated citizens, introducing them to the best that has been thought and said and helping to engender an appreciation of human creativity and achievement'. (OFSTED Framework, 2019). We must be mindful that we strike a meaningful balance because too much cognitive overload has a negative impact as discussed in Chapter 4 and so it is the well-sequenced curriculum that is critical to success.

Simple ideas for cultural capital (and these don't even scratch the surface but are straightforward for all schools to implement) that can be developed within your curriculum include the following:

- Visit the local library.
- Talk about the history of the local area.
- Utilize your university links and resources.
- Invite public speakers into the school.

- Utilize the expertise in local businesses.
- Develop a student speakers' programme.
- Introduce the family dining experience.
- A varied and enriched extra-curricular programme.
- All stakeholders use full sentences.
- A reader programme.

Social capital

Middle-class parents are more likely to hold university degrees and are more likely to help their children with homework and socialize their children with educational aspirations, for example, into thinking that going to university is the 'norm'. They therefore instil, through conversations early on, that good exam results are necessary. They tend to make informed choices about the school their child goes to, they will invest in reading OFSTED reports and looking at school results and performance tables. They are ultimately more in-tune with the education system itself. While we acknowledge that this is a sweeping generalization, it is something we must consider as schools if we are to address the disadvantage gap. It is vital, for example, that we ensure we have an excellent careers and education guidance programme, ensure that raising aspirations is embedded in our culture. Simple things such as making sure that non return of homework is addressed and supported, ensure we offer support through homework clubs and that we offer that extra-curricular experience as the 'norm'. We must also educate our parents – when we hear 'university isn't for my child', why not? What's the barrier? Is it financial? How can we guide them to the support that is on offer and ensure that everything is a possibility for their child? Young people with parents who have not attended university are found to be at a disadvantage with their likelihood for holding aspirations to pursue further study lowered by 31%. Our guidance is therefore critical to developing the social capital of all students (Social Mobility Commission, <https://assets.publishing.service.gov.uk/government/uploads/system/uploads/attachment_data/file/818679/An_Unequal_Playing_Field_report.pdf>).

One area we must consider in relation to aspirations are targets. Targets for children are an interesting source of debate and we should acknowledge that they can be a limiting factor in lots of respects. Targets add ceilings and can generate a feeling of 'not good enough' and can actively lower aspirations. For some children it can introduce mediocracy and an acceptance that, for example, getting a grade 4 is good enough because that was their target and they have achieved it. They can in some circumstances be damaging to the mental health of our students. Target grades can also generate complacency amongst the teaching profession – 'they've met their targets' or resentment in those data meetings 'they aren't meeting targets – why not?'. Schools can then be guilty of defining a student's ability by the ceiling set through an artificially generated target grade. Actually, we want all of our students to get the best possible grades that they can, and we should aspire to instil a culture within schools of 'wanting to get the best possible grades' and that comes from within – developing the culture to succeed; our social capital. Indeed, at many top independent schools you won't see a flight path or such equivalent glued into a student's book. Why? Because there is an expectation that we achieve the best that we can and there are and should be no ceilings or labels attached to that. There is an expectation in independent schools that students succeed academically and culturally. Social culture and social norms play a significant part in shaping this mindset.

Extra-curricular activities within the school system play a central role in developing social capital. The Unequal Playing Field report discusses the importance of enrichment activities and in particular through team work where positive social interactions are made. Accessibility to activities is vital to enrich life experiences, 'The breadth of extra-curricular activities, spanning the musical, artistic, social and sporting domains, are widely considered valuable life experiences that should be open to all young people, regardless of background or where they happen to live' (Social Mobility Commission, An Unequal Playing Field, <https://assets.publishing.service.gov.uk/government/uploads/system/uploads/attachment_data/file/818679/An_Unequal_Playing_Field_report.pdf>)

Extra-curricular activities are important in developing positive mental health. They expose students to new friendship groups, learning team skills, accepting loss as well as wins, and generally provide new skills and confidence. All children should be encouraged to take part in at least one extra-curricular activity per week and these are not all about sports clubs. Schools should be ambitious in their participation targets. They can include debate clubs, jewellery making, book clubs, music club, drama club, games club, archery club, science club, coding club, Duke of Edinburgh, charity club, and lots more. We recognize that in state schools the majority of extra-curricular provision tends to rely on teachers to run them and with the many demands on teachers currently in the profession this stretches resources even further for schools. In contrast independent schools are rich in extra-curricular opportunities. A study in 2014 showed that 42% of middle-class children took part in five or more extracurricular activities compared to 6.5% of working-class children. There was a high proportion of non-participation among their working-class participants, about 22% compared to 2% from children belonging to middle classes. If we are to narrow the gap and level the playing field, then surely this is something we need to consider? (Holloway & Pimlott-Wilson, 2014). Recent government initiatives play their part but need to go much further if we are to make a difference.

Participation in clubs outside of school for children from low-income households is challenged by the costs involved and other barriers can include confidence and simple things such as transport to the venue. 'There is evidence that extra-curricular activities play a prominent role in narrowing the inequality gap between advantaged and disadvantaged young people ... Structured school-based extra-curricular activities were associated with lower dropout rates, higher attainment levels and improved academic performance' (Social Mobility Commission, An Unequal Playing Field, <https://assets.publishing.service.gov.uk/government/uploads/system/uploads/attachment_data/file/818679/An_Unequal_Playing_Field_report.pdf>)

Mahoney and colleagues found that over time, consistent participation in structured extra-curricular activities has the potential to enhance students' motivation educationally, as well as set ambitious goals for their future, including those pertaining to education and career objectives (Mahoney et al., 2003). In turn, future intrinsic goal-framing has been shown to predict long-term persistence and better performance (Vansteenkiste et al., 2007). It is therefore important that schools provide those enrichment opportunities and encourage all students to participate; the impact on our young people could be far-reaching.

Developing social capital can also include very simple strategies such as family-style dining which encourages social norms and etiquette. Many students from disadvantaged backgrounds will eat their meals in front of the television and will not have experienced a formal dining setting. This style of dining encourages the art of conversation, and this is an important feature of developing social capital. It also supports positive mental health. Other factors which impact on mental health include the following with effect size listed (Visible Learning Plus. June, 2019):

Social, cultural, and educational capital

- Depression -0.26
- Anxiety -0.44
- Lack of sleep -0.05
- Boredom -0.47
- Lack of stress +0.17
- Bullying -0.20

It is therefore critical that our schools have an embedded mental health programme and there is a commitment to the mental health and well-being of students and staff.

Utilizing the resources at universities and taking students to visit the universities both locally and further afield allows students to broaden their horizons and visualize their next steps – we are making it a tangible experience and the concept of university no longer appears abstract or something they hear their teachers talk about. They have developed their schema, they have visited and experienced a university environment and begin to make connections.

Other very simple yet achievable ways to enhance social capital include visiting and teaching children how to use their local library. Not only does this support the literacy gain, but it is also a wonderful study area for students who have no quiet study zone or limited resources at home. Building up links with libraries and local museums is of positive benefit to schools as often they will loan artefacts which can be used in the classroom to enhance learning which provides cultural capital. There are lots of things that schools already do but the key to developing the capital from these activities is careful planning, monitoring, and quality assurance to determine the benefit for our students.

Educational capital

We provide educational capital through our curriculum and the entirety of this book is dedicated in many respects wholly to educational capital. When we begin to introduce social and cultural capital into our curriculum, we begin to make huge strides towards creating a truly inclusive curriculum and one where we are closing gaps. Our curriculum has integrity.

Social, cultural, and educational capital

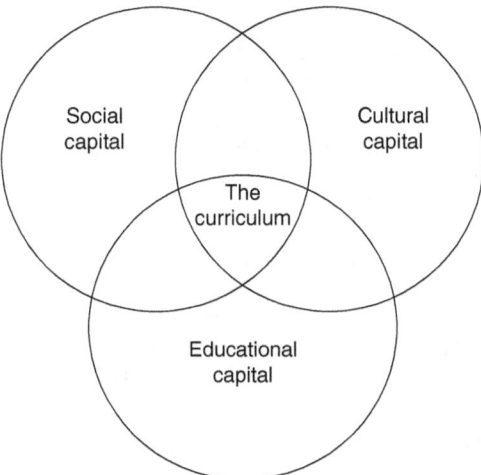

Figure 6.2 An empowered curriculum is formed when social, cultural, and educational capital combine

This isn't meant to be a magic wand but rather a think piece. Even small changes we make can make a big difference to the educational experiences of our students. These small changes must be well thought out and connected. Abstract or stand-alone points in a curriculum rarely have impact. It is better to do a small number of things (even one) properly and really embed practice consistently across the school than try to do everything badly or for subjects or other areas to do things in isolation (lacking connectedness). Figure 6.2 shows the connected approach we should visualize through our curriculum.

Schools can increase a student's educational capital by providing the best possible teaching and learning, setting high expectations, providing curricular materials, offering robust early intervention, mentoring programmes and ensuring that there is a cycle of assessment and review. Schools most likely already do all of these, and each provides educational capital, the connectedness is the key to impact.

Parents can support educational capital by ensuring their children attend school and that they complete home learning and attend parent events themselves, by simply being involved in and prioritizing their children's education. Students raised in families with low educational capital tend to view their futures with modest, if not pessimistic, expectations (MacLeod, 1994). This powerful relationship between home and school reinforces educational capital

Social, cultural, and educational capital

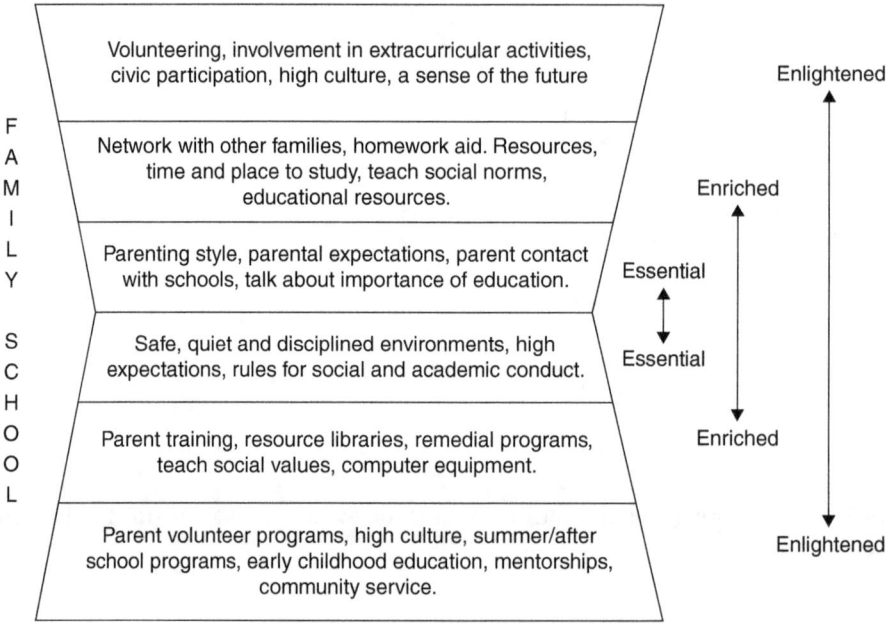

Figure 6.3 A schematic of the hierarchical model of educational capital (Howard et al., 1996)

as shown in Figure 6.3 and when we reach the enlightened phase, we gain optimization (Howard et al., 1996).

Summary

A key message from this chapter is that we must look closely at the combined impact of cultural, social, and educational capital on the outcomes of our students. The effect size provides us with further evidence for the impact on student learning (Hattie, 2009).

- Relations of high school to university achievement +0.60
- Enrichment programs +0.53
- Positive family/home dynamics +0.52
- Socio economic status +0.52

- Parental involvement +0.50
- Exposure to reading +0.43
- After school programs +0.40
- Out of school curricular experiences +0.26
- Family on welfare/state aid -0.12
- Moving between schools – 0.34

We should begin by ensuring all our staff understand what each term means. It is our responsibility to ensure in schools we provide the best possible opportunities through our curriculum to expose our students to the different forms of capital. Without staff having a clear understanding of what we mean and what we do not mean by the different forms of capital, the impact will be limited and may be negative.

The most important point to remember is that our curriculum can make a difference to the lives of the young people we teach. Our curriculum can open minds and open doors. Our curriculum matters and with a carefully crafted curriculum we become the architects of the future, we create truly meaningful opportunities for capital gain.

Checklist

- Do staff understand what we mean by social, cultural, and educational capital and has sufficient time been invested in professional development in this area?
- How does the golden thread of social and cultural capital weave through all areas of your school life, from your vision through to the individual lesson?
- How enriched is your programme of personal development?
- How does your school 'feel' when you walk around it? Does it 'feel' like a place of enriched social and cultural capital?
- What do your displays look like and how frequently do you change them?
- Does your strategic plan intrinsically promote social and cultural capital, for example, through your reading strategy?

Social, cultural, and educational capital

- Have you really ensured that your curriculum does not disadvantage the disadvantage and what is your litmus test for this; how do you know?
- Have you explored how you will involve parents in their child's education?
- Do all students participate in your extra-curricular activities?
- What does the analysis of students' 'next steps' show you in terms of their post 16 profiles or post 18 profiles?

Chapter 7

Quality assurance of the curriculum

We measure the quality of the curriculum through our assurance processes. These need to be specific and allow us to assess the impact of how well learners acquire and retain knowledge. Meaningful assurance processes must not only review the depth and breadth of the curriculum but look at the quality of implementation, the quality of student books and how well students can articulate their work and the outcomes of targeted assessments. The triangulation of these sources will provide us with a rich pool of information which will allow us to assure the quality of the curriculum. Careful consideration of each component is required to make a holistic judgement of quality. Looking at these elements in isolation will not provide a meaningful assessment of the curriculum.

By definition, quality assurance is a proactive measure which provides assurance that the high-quality outcomes (and this is not limited to or defined as assessment outcomes) we expect through our curriculum will be consistently achieved. It provides us with an overarching measure of confidence. This is not to be confused with a quality control process which is a reactive process that is operational and focuses on checking how well we fulfil the quality requirements within the curriculum based on output measures. The two, while often incorrectly used interchangeably, are quite distinct.

Quality assurance evolved from the manufacturing industry. Where individual sections or people were producing parts for an end point product, they had no control over the quality of the actual end point product itself which relied on the amalgamation of each of the respective components produced by various teams and only had control of the quality of their respective component. The factory would check a sample of completed end point products assuming that this was representative of all end point products and then control measures (quality control) were introduced to reduce defective items. Therefore, being a reactive process as it reacts to problems identified as a consequence of the end point measure. Quality assurance was introduced to prevent errors from occurring and not simply checking on end point products alone but the process itself 'along the way' looking at all component parts involved in producing the product. This is a proactive process. If we liken this to the school system then the quality control becomes our output measures and the quality assurance, for example, the process of learning walks or climate checks, the checking of books and learning conversations with our students, professional curriculum dialogue with our teachers. A potential pitfall, much likened to schools 'doing things for OFSTED', is that schools focus on compliance and there is a loss of creativity driving quality. Compliance with an external body can be detrimental to the collective drive to a vision. We must also ensure that those who are completing the quality assurance processes have adequate training and that quality assurance does not become compliant to a process. There is of course then the age-old conundrum of who inspects the inspector. In the UK we have internal and Trust level quality assurance, quality assurance through our governance models and quality assurance through regulatory bodies such as OFSTED. Keep in mind education is complex. Quality assessing in manufacturing is assessing the quality of an end point product that has very strict production criteria and all end point products should look the same measured against stringent standards for what the product should 'look like'. In schools we are dealing with people and our end point product for one student may be very different to the end point product for another.

The quality assurance cycle

Quality assurance should be mapped out throughout the course of the academic year and should be clearly communicated and understood by all stakeholders. In many schools there is a calendar of activities which may involve reviewing specific departments throughout the year. How these departments are decided on can be quite controversial because ultimately one department is left until towards the end of the year and most likely the decision is made based on quality control (outcome measures). This process doesn't necessarily work as well as perhaps looking at key themes across all departments over the academic year and then implementing a programme of deep dives that runs alongside this. This multi-pronged approach to quality assurance will be more effective in assuring the quality of the curriculum and allowing input into addressing any concerns much earlier on in the assurance cycle.

Quality assurance of the curriculum

All stakeholders need to be involved in the process: students, teaching assistants, teachers, middle leaders, senior leaders, and parents (often schools neglect parental voice as part of their quality assurance of the curriculum but collect it in relation to other aspects of school life; parent voice for the curriculum has a key part to play). We need to train our professional body of staff to become effective in the role. Without training the quality assurance process falls apart because to be meaningful it relies on consistency of process and consistency of judgement. We gain a measure of consistency through high-quality training and then ironically through quality assurance of the process we then implement. In other words, we need to quality assure the quality assurance process and you may rightly be thinking where does it all end.

We would advise that when you schedule your deep dives, this schedule will be informed by the outcomes of students and any concerns detected by the quality assurance processes over time. It is important that you communicate to staff that the calendar of deep dives is flexible, for example, your quality assurance processes may highlight a specific need and this may trigger a deep dive into a different subject to that which was scheduled. Some schools place deep dives on the calendar but do not inform staff of which subject it will be. The reasoning behind this is so that departments don't simply prepare for their deep dive (suddenly marking books for example) – in other words compliance to the assurance process. We would argue that if your quality assurance processes throughout the year are effective, such as your on-going learning walks across all subjects or your student book discussions, then this shouldn't happen. If you do still adopt this approach, one question I would advise you reflect on is about your role; is your role a supportive and developmental one (ultimately this culture leads to school improvements) or is it one where you try to 'catch people out'.

As shown in Figure 7.1 quality assurance is at every level within the school. Professionals in the classroom (and this includes both teachers and teaching assistants) begin by assuring the quality of their delivery of the curriculum and they do this through the feedback and marking process as well as through observational notes and targeted questioning. The most powerful part of this is when teachers engage in individual or small group learning discussions with their students. These can be driven by areas where student books showed a lack of understanding and learning conversations allow teachers to unpick any misconceptions or potential areas where the curriculum may disadvantage certain groups of students and feed this back at department level for potential

Quality assurance of the curriculum

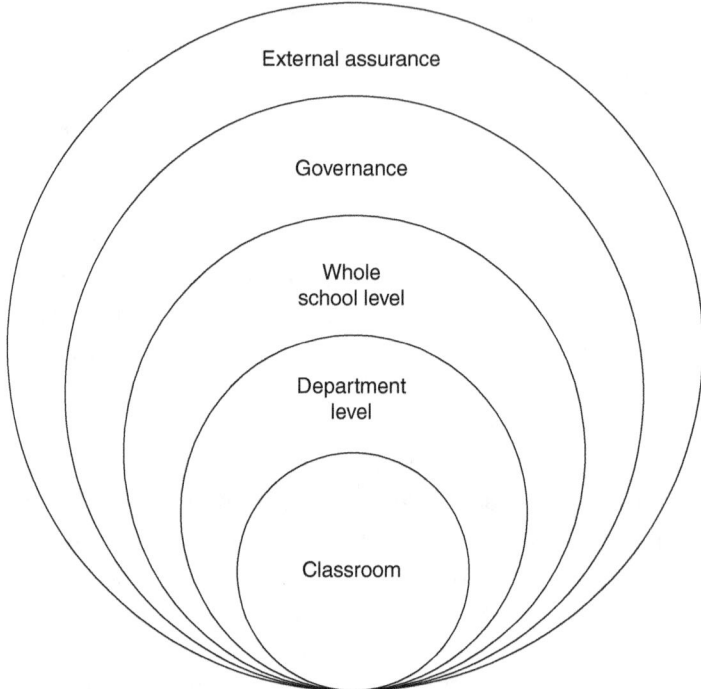

Figure 7.1 Quality assurance at every level within the school

curriculum review. This is an extremely powerful part of the quality assurance process but involves schools investing in training for their staff to develop them as reflective practitioners. It is not something we can assume people know how to do simply because 'they are a teacher'.

At middle leader level, for example, Head of Department (HOD) level, we would expect that data informs sampling and that when looking at student books a HOD may look at students who are achieving above expected, at expected, or below expected standards. They may be interested in focusing on a particular group, such as SEND or disadvantaged students. Their role is the first layer of 'checking' outside of the classroom and will encompass learning walks, book reviews and student learning conversations and conversations with individual teachers discussing the findings from their assurances as well as the curriculum conversations. It will also involve quality assurance through standardization and moderation to ensure that the data is accurate in the first place. Perhaps the most critical stage of this layer is feeding back to the department and then working as a collective to take a measured response when using the quality assurance process to review the curriculum and the quality of provision. Without this phase the process is irrelevant and simply a 'tick box' exercise. Remember quality assurance is the process of assessing the quality of the component parts to ensure the end point product improves. In our cases the end point products are the acquisition of knowledge of all learners through the vehicle of the curriculum and if the vehicle requires maintenance, we need to involve our curriculum team in this process as, in reference to the manufacturing analogy, they are 'producing the components' that go together to make the final product.

At senior leader level we are quality assuring the process at department level and have a larger field from which to sample. Senior leaders may be responsible for several departments and so will gain a holistic view of consistency. This level of quality assurance introduces the 'mass production phase'. Rather than focusing on 30 students in a class we are now scaled up to 300 in a year and across line management of three subjects, potentially 900 input points. This means identifying the right components is very important. Furthermore, senior leaders may not be subject specialists in the areas they line manage and so we face the first layer of the 'quality of inspector' conundrum and need to ensure that we are not simply assessing compliance to a process or set of strict criteria. It is therefore the quality of the conversations with the HOD that form a vital part of the process whereupon the subject specialism of the HOD is used to support the assurance while maintaining robust professional challenge through line management. At the same time this offers a learning conversation for the HOD and so we see a cycle of professional development.

When we move to the senior leader responsible for curriculum and the Headteacher we are truly on 'mass scale production' and so we need to ensure that our quality assurance at all layers before this phase are robust. For a school of 900 students with, for example, 10 subjects studied by each student there are 9000 student books, 9000 end point measures at each phase of assessment, 60 classes per year and 300 classes across the school. Therefore, we are quality assuring the quality assurance process at senior leader level and Headteachers rely heavily on the quality of the phases that come before them.

Governance layers tend to judge a 'snapshot' and this can involve climate checks alongside regular (typically monthly or half termly) reporting measures which can include summary judgements on the quality of teaching and student outcomes. External quality assurance is completed by agencies such as OFSTED who will make an overarching judgement about the quality of provision and this process is a short visit, typically 2 days once every few years (depending on the judgement of the school).

Quality assurance of the curriculum

The most critical part of this process is staff training. If, for example, a middle leader cannot effectively assess the quality of learning against the curriculum then the assurance process falls apart. Headteachers need to be confident that all staff can complete their phase of the process with confidence, at the required level and consistently.

Key questions to ask yourselves

- When did we last train teachers to assess learning against the curriculum?
- How do we know our learning walks are completed with purpose and consistently?
- How do we know our student learning conversations are asking the right questions?
- How do we know our quality assurance process is improving the student learning experience?

Quality of implementation

We are looking to check that there is curriculum continuity because the curriculum, by definition, is a continual development of learner knowledge, strong subject expertise or curriculum knowledge and well-sequenced learning across year groups, key stages and progressive development vertically (spiral development through the years) and horizontally (across a year group) within the subject-specific environment.

When we assess the quality of implementation, we are ultimately assessing how well the curriculum is brought to life within the classroom environment with the best impact on learner knowledge. We cannot do this in a single observation or learning walk. This is much deeper than that and must involve self-reflective practitioners as well as peer and line management reviews. Often the latter is achieved through learning walks, however, you should ask yourselves whether learning walks are purposeful.

Do your learning walks:

- Result in high-quality curriculum conversations which lead to department discussions about the quality of provision.
- Always involve curriculum discussions with the class teacher which probe the teacher's subject knowledge and understanding.

Quality assurance of the curriculum

- Always involve learning conversations with a sample of students.
- Always use the curriculum in hand when completing the learning walk.
- Have a flexible approach that allows the HOD to be relieved from teaching so they can see each of their team across a range of groups.
- Adopt a paired approach at random to assure the judgements and allow assurance conversations (this may be two middle leaders or a middle leader and a senior leader or a middle leader and a responsibility holder within the subject team).

Or do your learning walks:

- Result in a judgement on an excel spreadsheet (or equivalent tracker).
- Tell you what you already know about the 'quality of teaching'.
- Rarely find time for a learning conversation with the class teacher or students.
- Involve 'flicking through a student book' to see if it appears to meet a set criteria of standards.
- Fail to result in curriculum challenge or meaningful discussion with the department team.
- Follow a timetable and are only possible when the HOD is not teaching which means that your HOD always sees the same teachers with the same classes.
- Rely on one person doing the learning walks to make sure they are all done so that on the 'recording system' we meet compliance.

If it is the last set of bullet points, then we operate a compliance system that will not lead to improvements or at least not the improvements we want to see. If we operate the first set of bullet points, we operate an assurance system and we will see cultural change and transformation at all levels.

So, how do we conduct a meaningful learning walk? The first phase is to 'know' the curriculum and where the composite fits into the component and where the component fits into the long-term plan. This was discussed in detail in Chapters 2 and 3, and here we simply acknowledge the importance of all stakeholders in this phase but, in particular, senior leaders who may not be the subject specialists. They must understand the curriculum sequence of the areas they line manage and be able to provide the professional challenge, otherwise the learning walks focus on compliance, checking, for example, if the starter was knowledge retrieval, was there effective questioning and so on. All of this is extremely important but of course it is only impactful in the context of the curriculum rather than an abstract skill in its own right. You can go into a lesson and see brilliant questioning or an activity which on the surface seems to be engaging, but the key is to dig deep and determine if the questions being asked are about the right thing to drive learning and develop schema and if the activity is the best activity to optimize learning and maximize powerful knowledge. Transformation then happens; learning walks go beyond making the superficial judgements we tend to see of red, amber, green or A, B, C, D or outstanding, good, requires improvement or inadequate to learning walks that promote a culture of development and a culture with learning at its core.

When we conduct a learning walk, the powerful knowledge that the students are expected to acquire during the lesson will be identified on the curriculum documentation and this will be our starting point. Of course, we will be looking at the teacher's behaviour management, the quality of modelling and scaffolding, questioning technique and so on but this would form part of a wider context about generic pedagogy. Specifically, we are looking at the lesson as a vehicle to deliver the curriculum and will be focusing on the quality of learning over time of which the learning walk forms one piece of the puzzle. We will be identifying how well powerful knowledge is delivered and embedded.

When we have the peer learning conversation with the teacher, we may have two foci: the pedagogical approach and the curriculum learning. Here we address the curriculum learning and we engage discussions on:

- How well does the teacher understand where the lesson fits within the composite and how learning is developed?
- How well do they understand the long-term plan and where the learning fits within this?
- Can the teacher explain the sequencing and provide a specific example?
- Can the teacher demonstrate the powerful knowledge that students must learn to be successful?
- Can the teacher identify the tier 3 vocabulary?
- Does the teacher identify the key steps in the modelling process?
- Does the teacher have an awareness of potential misconceptions and how pitfalls will be overcome?

Making time for these discussions is key to changing the culture of an organization and time is often identified as the main barrier. One question to ask leaders is whether the current professional development you deliver (most likely an hour a week) is having the desired impact. If you are seeing transformational learning and a common language in your school with strong stakeholder buy-in, then the answer to this will be 'yes'. However, most likely you are not and the most important thing you can do is reflect on the use of this dedicated development time. Probably the most effective action you could take is to allocate this time to the curriculum. Depending on the stage you are at, this might be curriculum development or it may be the quality assurance process where you facilitate the learning conversations. This will bring maximum benefit to your academy and will begin to transform your culture to a culture of learning.

Student learning conversations

Student learning conversations, whether during the learning walk or as soon as possible after the learning walk, will form one of the best bases for reviewing the effectiveness of the lesson. These should be conducted with the student or a small group of students and their books.

Key elements we should focus on:

- What do the students remember from the work in their books today, the previous lesson, lessons a week ago, lessons at the start of the term, and how is this learning connected? In other words, we are checking if the students can articulate a sequence to their learning and we are checking how well our curriculum develops schema.

- What do we think the next steps in our learning could be? This is an opportunity to gauge the level of contextual understanding the student has acquired and their level of connected thinking.

One thing this is not is a compliance check. Very often book 'checks' will be completed by going through the students' books without ever having a learning conversation with the student themselves. All this does is tell us that the book complies with standards. Even if we do this exercise with the curriculum document next to us, all it will tell us is how well or how badly a teacher has followed the curriculum. It tells us very little about the students' understanding and indeed they could have copied everything off the board. We refer to my original statement: everything should have a purpose. If your purpose is standards checks then this is a perfectly acceptable exercise. If your purpose is to check the impact of your curriculum this exercise falls short of achieving this objective and must be done with the student present to allow a learning conversation.

During the conversation with the student some key questions should be posed, and it is important to complete this exercise under a framework in which all staff have had training. Similarly, students will need training, and this may be through an assembly about why we do this process and what we expect from them.

When we are talking to students during a lesson, we need to focus on whether the student understands the specific task itself and why they are doing it. We would be looking to see if students can make any connections at this point, for example, 'last lesson we did this and so this fits in here because…'. We would be expecting the student to be able to illustrate this with their books. You may choose to ask students about a piece of feedback. Have they read the feedback and how has this allowed them to improve? Have they participated in the process and is there an opportunity for further review? How do they know they have now secured this area of the curriculum?

When we talk to students outside of the lesson itself (and with their books) we can ask the same questions in greater depth and discuss specific examples or follow a more rigorous line of enquiry. This gives us the opportunity to 'assess the curriculum' in greater depth.

A framework for discussion is outlined below:

- Can you tell me what the lesson was about?

- What was the key knowledge you need to know?

- Can you give me an example of how the work from the previous lesson has helped you in this lesson?

- How do you know?

- When was this unit of work started?

- Is this the first time you have seen this topic? (This may lead to a discussion about work completed in the previous year, for example where you can probe memory retrieval.)

- How does it build on the previous unit of work – are there any connections between X and Y?

Quality assurance of the curriculum

The questions will develop naturally but there should always be a common framework as the purpose is to support curriculum development and for the subject team to use the findings of the student learning conversation as part of their curriculum review. This will combine with measures of student outcomes to determine the impact of the curriculum.

Summary

Arguably, the most impactful parts of the quality assurance process are the learning conversations that happen. The information we glean from this dialogue should inform our curriculum reviews and this must be an intrinsic part of the process. Curriculum development is a cycle, as illustrated in Figure 7.2, which involves assessment of our implantation phase, and this 'data' informs our review. The cycle then begins again with the aim of developing a rich and diverse curriculum which develops the knowledge and schema of the learner.

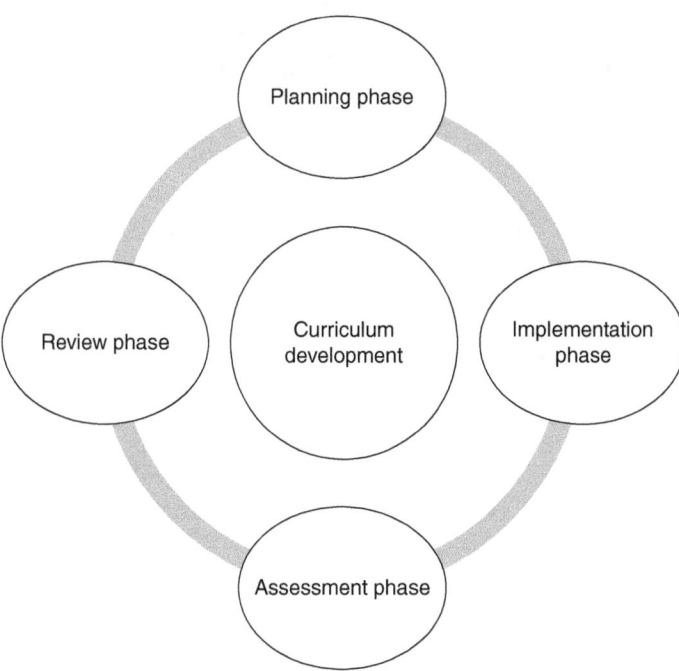

Figure 7.2 A cycle of curriculum development informed by the quality assurance process

Quality assurance of the curriculum

Checklist

- Do staff understand the processes of quality assurance and quality control?
- Have you invested in staff training and development?
- Have your processes been clearly communicated to stakeholders and do they understand their role?
- Do you have well-defined impact measures?
- Is leadership dissipated to ensure highly effective quality assurance at all levels?
- Is there a calendar of quality assurance and has this been implemented strategically?
- Is your quality assurance looking at the right things and how do you know?
- What do you do with the information from your quality assurance processes?
- How does your quality assurance inform your strategic planning and your evaluation process at whole school, department, and class teacher level?

Conclusion

Curriculum development is an ongoing and continuous cycle of review. It is a multifaceted process and underpins the very core purpose of our schools. In this final chapter we aim to provide you with a simple step-by-step guide to beginning your curriculum conversations.

As discussed in Chapter 1, without a whole school vision your curriculum lacks purpose. Your first step is to understand the whole school vision and how this vision will be brought to life through subject curriculum. When you develop the subject vision you should identify:

- Why do students study your subject?
- What is truly inspiring about your subject?
- What key skills and transferable skills do students develop through your subject?
- How does it feed into the wider world?
- How will the whole school values thread through the subject curriculum?

The subject vision forms an integral part of the curriculum intent. Key questions to support the development of the intent statement:

- Does the subject vision align with the whole school vision?
- Is the rationale for sequencing the curriculum clear?
- Does the sequencing of the curriculum provide optimum conditions for students to activate prior knowledge to develop new knowledge?

Conclusion

- Are the content choices ambitious? They should be at least as challenging as the national curriculum.

- Are the 'powerful knowledge' or threshold concepts of your curriculum clearly articulated?

As discussed in Chapter 2 the high-level plan is developed with careful consideration of the sequencing of knowledge both horizontally and vertically throughout the curriculum. The high-level plan should consider:

- Is there a clear link between the intent statement and the high-level plan?

- Is the content outlined in the intent statement evident in the high-level plan?

- Is the curriculum sequenced as outlined in the intent statement?

- Can you clearly identify the threshold concepts or powerful knowledge of the curriculum?

- Is there evidential progression?

- Is the rationale for assessment of the curriculum clear?

- Are the end points of the curriculum identified and do they take account of and develop from the end points of the previous curriculum phase? How do the end points enable transition to the next phase of learning?

In Chapter 3 we outlined how to deconstruct composite knowledge into the component parts. This is where is we really begin to provide a framework for progressive learning and where we ensure our curriculum is accessible for all students:

- Have you identified the end point for the composite knowledge?

- Have you broken down the composite knowledge into the component knowledge and ensured this is well sequenced?

- Have you ensured component knowledge is specific?

- Have you identified the knowledge needed for scaffolding?

- Have you identified the opportunities for students to deepen their knowledge?

- Have you identified the tier 2 and 3 vocabularies for each component?

Conclusion

Implementation of the curriculum is through our learning episodes and where we focus on the impact of pedagogy on the student learning experience. In Chapter 4 we discussed the importance of the learning cycle in the context of cognitive load and how we need to reduce variability and develop consistency across our teaching teams. When developing a lesson, it is important to consider:

- Have you taken the curriculum content and identified the powerful knowledge?
- Have you ensured learning is well sequenced?
- Have you identified the development of skills?
- Is cognitive load central to your planning?
- Have you maximized germane load, minimized extraneous load, and managed intrinsic load?
- Is planning meticulous to account for dual coding?
- Have you carefully selected the Big Question based on the four most important knowledge points?
- Have you ensured a focus on literacy and used the Frayer model to decode?
- Does your learning cycle use the I do, we do, you do model to scaffold and support learning?
- Have you identified sensory input?
- Have you carefully considered the questions you will ask and the level of question along with possible misconceptions?
- Have you considered how you will 'know' learning has happened?
- Have you completed a walk with a focus on the learning environment?

Assessment of the curriculum allows us to address the 'how do you know?'. It forms a critical part of our cycle of curriculum review and continuous improvement. Chapter 5 discussed the intricacies of assessment, some key points for consideration:

- Are your assessments carefully mapped and aligned to the curriculum?
- What form of assessment is most appropriate for the curriculum knowledge?

Conclusion

- How are you assessing both substantive and disciplinary knowledge?
- Have you checked the suitability of the questions to ensure you are getting the right information from the students?
- How are you going to provide feedback?
- Through what medium will you deliver feedback?
- How are you going to integrate re-testing into the curriculum?
- How are you going to review the relevant composite and any linked curriculum based on the triangulation of assessment data, student and staff voice, student workbook reviews, and implementation reviews?
- An effective curriculum review of the medium-term plan may include:
  - Compliance checks on whether there is evidence that all the component knowledge was covered in the curriculum.
  - What misconceptions the students had during the teaching of the component, identified through assessment, student and staff voice and student workbooks.
  - The effectiveness and impact of scaffolding.
  - How well students' knowledge of disciplinary knowledge is being developed across the curriculum.
  - Any variation in student indicators such as SEND or disadvantaged students.

Capital is a broad term that gives value or advantage and our curriculum as a learning tool should be more than 'what students will know'. With careful consideration of social, cultural, and education capital we will begin to address gaps in cohort learning. Chapter 6 discusses the different types of capital and their relevance to learning. Key points to consider are:

- Do staff understand what we mean by social, cultural, and educational capital and has sufficient time been invested in professional development in this area?
- How does the golden thread of social and cultural capital weave through all areas of your school life, from your vision through to the individual lesson?

Conclusion

- How enriched is your programme of personal development?
- How does your school 'feel' when you walk around it? Does it 'feel' like a place of enriched social and cultural capital?
- What do your displays look like and how frequently do you change them?
- Does your strategic plan intrinsically promote social and cultural capital, for example, through your reading strategy?
- Have you really ensured that your curriculum does not disadvantage the disadvantaged and what is your litmus test for this; how do you know?
- Have you explored how you will involve parents in their child's education?
- Do all students participate in your extra-curricular activities?
- What does the analysis of students' 'next steps' show you in terms of their post 16 profiles or post 18 profiles?

We measure the quality of the curriculum through our assurance process. Quality assurance is a proactive measure which provides assurance that the high quality we expect throughout our curriculum is consistently achieved. In Chapter 7 we discussed how this provides us with an overarching measure of confidence in our curriculum. Quality assurance considerations include:

- Do staff understand the processes of quality assurance and quality control?
- Have you invested in staff training and development?
- Have your processes been clearly communicated to stakeholders and do they understand their role?
- Do you have well-defined impact measures?
- Is leadership dissipated to ensure highly effective quality assurance at all levels?
- Is there a calendar of quality assurance and has this been implemented strategically?
- Is your quality assurance looking at the right things and how do you know?
- What do you do with the information from your quality assurance processes?

Conclusion

- How does your quality assurance inform your strategic planning and your evaluation process at whole school, department, and class teacher level?

Developing the curriculum is a complex process and one that requires significant investment of time and resources. This book has provided an overview of the process of curriculum development from the whole school vision to the individual learning episodes. We hope that it has provided you with useful discussion points within your schools and that it has acted in the very least as a think piece for your curriculum development.

Bibliography

Anderson, L.W. and Krathwohl, D.R. (Eds). (2001). *A Taxonomy for Learning, Teaching and Assessing: A Revision of Bloom's Taxonomy of Educational Objectives: Complete Edition*. New York: Longman.

Atkinson, R.C. and Shiffrin, R.M. (1968). *Human Memory: A Proposed System and Its Control Processes; The Psychology of Learning and Motivation Vol 2*. New York: New York Academic Press, pp. 89–195.

Bartlett, J. (2015a). *Outstanding Assessment for Learning*. London: Routledge.

Bartlett, J. (2015b). *Outstanding Differentiation for Learning*. London: Routledge.

Beck, I., McKeown, M., and Kucan, L. (2002). *Bringing Words to Life: Robust Vocabulary Instruction*. New York: The Guildford Press.

Bloom, B.S. (1956). *Taxonomy of Educational Objectives. Vol. 1: Cognitive domain*. New York: McKay, pp. 20, 24.

Bordieu, P. (2010). *Distinction*. London: Routledge.

Bruner, J.S. (1960). *The Process of Education*. Boston, MA: Harvard University Press.

Bruner, J.S. (1966). *Toward a Theory of Instruction*. Boston, MA: Harvard University Press.

Cook, G. (1997) Key concepts in ELT: Schemas. *ELT Journal*, 5(1): 86.

Cotton, K. (1988). Classroom questioning. School Improvement Research Series (p. 6).

Cowan, N. (2010). The Magical Mystery Four: How is working memory capacity limited, and why? *Current Directions in Psychological Science*, 1 February, 19(1): 51–57.

Cousin, G. (2006). An introduction to threshold concepts. *Planet*, 17(1): 4–5.

Dickens, C. (1992). *Oliver Twist*. Wordsworth Editions, ISBN: 9781853260124.

Donovan, S. and Bransford, J. (2005). *How Students Learn: History, Mathematics, and Science in the Classroom*. Washington, DC: National Academies Press.

Ebbinghaus, H. (1885). *Über das Gedächtnis: Untersuchungen zur experimentellen Psychologie*. Leipzig: Duncker & Humblot.

Efland, A. (1995). The Spiral and the Lattice: Changes in Cognitive Learning Theory with implications for art education. *Studies in Art Education*, 36(3): 134–153.

Bibliography

Gambrell, L.B. and Morrow, L.M. (2015). *Best Practices in Literacy Instruction* (5th Edition). New York: The Guilford Press.

Hattie, J. (2009). *Visible Learning: A Synthesis of over 800 Meta-analyses Relating to Achievement.* London and New York: Routledge.

Harris, T.L. and Hodges, R.E. (1995). *The Literacy Dictionary.* Newark, DE: International Reading Association.

Holloway, S.L. and Pimlott-Wilson, H. (2014). Enriching children, institutionalizing childhood? Geographies of play, extra-curricular activities, and parenting in England. *Annals of the Association of American Geographers*, 104(3): 613–627.

Howard, V.F., MacLaughlin, T.F., and Vacha, E.F. (1996). Educational capital: A proposed model and its relationship to academic and social behaviour of students at risk. *Journal of Behavioural Education*, 6(2), June, 135–152.

Kasper, L.J., Alderson, R.M., and Hudec, K.L. (2012). Moderators of working memory deficits in children with attention-deficit/hyperactivity disorder (ADHD): A meta-analytic review. *Clinical Psychology Review*, 32(7): 606–614.

Kirschner, P.A., Sweller, J., and Clark, R.E. (2006). Why minimal guidance during instruction does not work: An analysis of the failure of constructivist discovery, problem-based, experiential, and inquiry-based teaching. *Educational Psychologist*, 41(2): 75–86.

Leslie, K., Low, R., Jin, P., and Sweller, J. (2012). Redundancy and expertise reversal effects when using educational technology to learn primary school science. *Educational Technology Research and Development*, 60(1): 1–13.

Levin, T. and Long, R. (1981). *Effective Instruction.* Alexandria, VA: Association for Supervision and Curriculum Development.

MacLeod, J. (1994). *Ain't Makin' It: Levelled Aspirations in a Low Income Neighborhood* (2nd edn). Boulder, CO: Westview Press.

Mahoney, J.L., Cairns, B.D., and Farmer, T.W. (2003). Promoting interpersonal competence and educational success through extra-curricular activity participation. *Journal of Educational Psychology*, 95(2): 409.

Mehta, J. and Fine, S. (2019). *In Search of Deeper Learning: The Quest to Remake the American High School.* Boston, MA: Harvard University Press.

Meyer, J.H.F. and Land, L. (2005). Threshold concepts and troublesome knowledge (2): Epistemological considerations and conceptual framework for teaching and learning. *High Education*, 49: 373–388.

Ofsted (2021). *Research Review Series: Science.* Available at: www.gov.uk/government/publications/research-review-series-science/research-review-series-science (Accessed: 4 December 2022).

Pachman, M., Sweller, J., and Kalyuga, S. (2013). Levels of knowledge and deliberate practice. *Journal of Experimental Psychology: Applied*, 19(2): 108–119.

Peterson, R. (1992). Understanding audience segmentation: From elite and mass to omnivore and univore. *Poetic*, 21: 243–258.

Sweller, J. (2016). Story of a research program. *Education Review*, 23: 1–18.

Sweller, J., van Merrienboer, J.J.G., and Paas, F.G.W.C. (1998). Cognitive architecture and instructional design. *Educational Psychology Review*, 10(3): 251–296.

The National Curriculum (2018). London: SAGE.

Vansteenkiste, M., Matos, L., Lens, W., and Soenens, B. (2007). Understanding the impact of intrinsic versus extrinsic goal framing on exercise performance: The conflicting role of task and ego involvement. *Psychology of Sport and Exercise*, 8(5): 771–794.

Webb, M. and Jones, J. (2009) Exploring tensions in developing assessment for learning. *Assessment in Education: Principles, Policy & Practice*, 16(2): 165–184.

Yeung, A., Jin, P., and Sweller, J. (1998). Cognitive load and learner expertise: Split attention and redundancy effects in reading with explanatory notes. *Contemporary Educational Psychology*, 23(1): 1–21.

Young, M. (2008) *Review of Research in Education*, 32: 1–28.

Young, M., Lambert, D., and Roberts, C. (2014) *Knowledge and the Future School: Curriculum and Social Justice*. London: Bloomsbury.

Electronic Resources

BBC Bitesize, www.bbc.co.uk/bitesize [accessed on 5 December 2022].

Bjork, E.L. and Bjork, R. (2011) Making things hard on yourself, but in a good way: Creating desirable difficulties to enhance learning, <https://bjorklab.psych.ucla.edu/wp-content/uploads/sites/13/2016/04/EBjork_RBjork_2011.pdf#:~:text=So%20what%20are%20these%20better%20conditions%20of%20learning,and%20usingtests%2C%20rather%20than%20presentations%2C%20as%20study%20events> [accessed on 28 November 2022].

Centre for Education Statistics and Evaluation (2017). *Cognitive load theory:* Research that teachers really need to understand, September 2017, Centre for Education Statistics and Evaluation, Australia, <www.cesa.nswa.gov.au/images/stories/PDF/cognitive-load-theory-VR_AA3.pdf> [accessed 8 July 2022].

Counsell, C. (2018a). 'Taking curriculum seriously', Impact (4). <https://my.charteredcollege/impact_article/taking-curriculum-seriously/> [accessed on 4 December 2022].

Counsell, C. (2018b) *'Senior Curriculum Leadership 1:* The indirect manifestation of knowledge: (A) curriculum as narrative', The dignity of the thing, 7 April 2018 [Blog]. https://thedignityofthethingblog.wordpress.com/2018/04/07/senior-curriculum-leadership-1-the-indirect-manifestation-of-knowledge-a-curriculum-as-narrative/ [accessed on 4 December 2022].

Education Endowment Foundation (EEF) (2021a). Education Endowment Foundation, <https://d2tic4wvo1iusb.cloudfront.net/eef-guidance-reports/literacy-ks3-ks4/EEF_KS3_KS4_LITERACY_GUIDANCE.pdf?v=1670402473> (First uploaded October 2021) [accessed on 13 December 2022].

Education Endowment Foundation (EEF) (2021b). https://educationendowmentfoundation.org.uk/education-evidence/teaching-learning-toolkit/feedback [accessed on 15 November 2022].

International Dyslexia Association <https://dyslexiada.org/working-memory-the-engine-for-learning/> [accessed on 12 October 2022].

Meyer, J.H.F and Land, R. (2003). Threshold concepts and troublesome knowledge: Linkages to ways of thinking and practising with the disciplines. Occasional report 4. www.etl.tla.ed.ac.uk/docs/ETLreport4.pdf [accessed on 3 December 2022].

Bibliography

National Literacy Trust. <https://literacytrust.org.uk/parents-and-families/adult-literacy/> [accessed on 10 December 2022].

OFSTED Framework. (2019). Education inspection framework (EIF) – *GOV.UK* (<www.gov.uk>) [accessed on 15 July 2022].

OFSTED Research Review Series: Science www.gov.uk/government/publications/research-review-series-science/research-review-series-science [accessed on 4 September 2022].

Social Mobility Commission. *An Unequal Playing Field*, <https://assets.publishing.service.gov.uk/government/uploads/system/uploads/attachment_data/file/818679/An_Unequal_Playing_Field_report.pdf> [accessed on 4 December 2022].

The National Theatre. <www.nationaltheatre.org.uk/learning/national-theatre-collection/uk-state-funded-schools> [accessed on 4 August 2022].

Visible Learning Plus. (June, 2019). 250+ Influences on Student Achievement. Thousand Oaks, CA: Corwin Press. Retrieved from: <https://us.corwin.com/sites/default/files/250_influences_chart_june_2019.pdf> [accessed on 7 September 2022].

Visible Learning. *Hattie Effect Size List – 256 Influences Related To Achievement (visible-learning.org)* <https://visible-learning.org/hattie-ranking-influences-effect-sizes-learning-achievement/> [accessed on 20 August 2022].

William, D. (2011). *What Assessment Can – and Cannot – Do.* www.dylanwiliam.org link to article: <https://view.officeapps.live.com/op/view.aspx?src=http%3A%2F%2Fwww.dylanwiliam.org%2FDylan_Wiliams_website%2FPapers_files%2FPedagogiska%2520magasinet%2520article.docx&wdOrigin=BROWSELINK> [accessed on 13 September 2022].

Index

Note: Page locators in **bold** and *italics* represents tables and figures, respectively.

6 week half term cycle 85
256 Influences Related To Achievement 48, 102

algebraic processes 72
algebraic skills 17
argue filtering 50
art of conversation 111
'assumed' knowledge 37
automation, process of 52–3, 55–6

basic memory 63–4
Bell, Alexander Graham 16, 23
Benz, Carl 16, 23
Big Question 59–65, 71, 78, 79, 82, 131
Bloom's taxonomy of cognition 40, 76
Bourdieu, Pierre 101
Bruner, J.S. 8, 21

calculations, process-driven 55
capital gain: cultural and social 101; opportunities for 115; principles of 101
card sorting activities 64
class question level analysis 92
classroom environment 79–81, 124
cognitive load 69; basics of 49–51; implications for teacher planning 72; and learning in the main 65–6; scaffolding 71; theory of 45, 47, 62; types of 55–6
cognitive processing 71
cognitive questions: higher-order 75–6; lower-order 75
cognitive science 9, 12
cognitive theory 8
cognitive theory of multimedia learning (CTML) 56
colour-coded storage system 54
'common sense' knowledge 10
communication techniques, subject-specific 42
component knowledge 30, 91; chains of 80; GCSE-style science question 88; summary of 89
composite and component structure 18–19
composite assessment: creating an 86–7; interim and end of 83–5; length of 85; selecting the right questions 87–89; through the learning cycle 85
composite knowledge 30; breaking down of 30–4; summary of 86
conceptual knowledge 98–9

Index

content knowledge 9, 16, 18, 20, 22, 30, 90, 105
continuity and change, concept of 16, 19
core knowledge 34, 86
Counsell, Christine 34
creativity, virtue of 48
cross-curricular learning 37
cultural capital: development of 3, 101–3; Frayer model 105; impact of learning 37; impact on student' progress 11; knowledge and 105–9; literacy and 103–5; OFSTED Framework (2019) 108; sources of 101; as tool to transform learning 108
cultural development 103
culture of learning 125
curriculum: conversations 8, 26, 120, 122, 129; documentation 21, 124; hierarchy 15; learners 12; learning 92–3, 124–5; organizational tools 25; quality of 61; sequencing 5, 22
curriculum development 8–9, 12, 60, 127, 129; aim of 16; composite and component structure 18–19; cycle of *127*; high-level plan 15–18, 19–22, 27; history intent statement (extract) 16; levels of 27; long-term subject plan 15; maths intent 15–18; medium-term planning 22; phases of 15; quality assuring the long-term plan 25–6; role of memory in 22–5; subject intent statement *versus* high-level plan *23*
curriculum intent, development of 9–12
curriculum knowledge 9–10, 12, 19, 22, 86, 92; categories of 30–1; deconstructing of 34–7; determination of 10; development of 30; gaps in 97–8; identifying *33*; revisiting 22–5
curriculum models 4, 7, 11–12, 14; composite and component 12; interleaved 25; lattice model 8; network 1; spaced 27; spiral 1, 25, 27; types of 8

declarative knowledge 31, 87
deepen understanding, opportunities to 39–41, *42*
deeper learning 8, 48, 101
disadvantaged student analysis 92
disciplinary knowledge 31, 87, 99, 100, 132
disciplinary literacy 42; acquisition of 87; in art *43*; development of *43*; teaching of 42
dual coding 56–7, 64, 68, 82, 131
dyslexia 50

Ebbinghaus, Hermann 22; forgetting curve *24*, 25
educational capital 3, 112–14; hierarchical model of *114*
education guidance programme 109
Efland, A. 8
episodic memory 51
experiential learning 106
extra-curricular activities 110–11, 133
extraneous load 55–6, 80, 82, 98–9, 131

feedback 83, 85, 87, 91–3, *94*, 97, 119, 126, 132
food technology, opportunities to deepen understanding in *41*, 42, 86, 108
forgetting curve, development of 22, *24*, 25
Frayer model, for development of literacy decoding 105, *106*, 131

germane load 56; 'I do, we do, you do' cycle 66
German interim assessment: reading 84; writing 84
Google Earth 106–7

Hattie, John 48, 66, 102
Head of Department (HOD) 120
high-level plan, for curriculum development 16–17, 19–2, 26
hinterland knowledge 34, 86
history intent statement 16

Index

horizontal development, of school curriculum 8

identity, virtue of 48
'I do, we do, you do' cycle 66
impact sequencing 21
implementation of the curriculum 25, 131
implementation, quality of 122–5
information processing 49, *52*, 56
instruction 21
instructional failure 71
interactive skills 104
interleaved curriculum 25
interpretive skills 104
intrinsic load 55–6, 131

job market 103

key questions, in developing the vision and mission of school curriculum 7
knowledge: acquisition of 121; common sense 10; concept of 34; construction of 12; core 34; and cultural capital 105–9; curriculum *see* curriculum knowledge; declarative 31; development of 8, 46; disciplinary 31; interconnectivity of 21; powerful 10; procedural knowledge 31–3; process-driven 47; recall and retrieval on retention 22; for scaffolding 37–9; sequencing of 30; structure 21; substantive 32; of Victorian Britain (History curriculum) 37
knowledge gaps 37, 83, 85, 87, 92, 97; re-testing in case of 98–9
knowledge retrieval 62, 64, 98, 124; benchmarking of 64–5
knowledge selection and sequencing, importance of 12
knowledge 'success', acquisition of 60

labelling diagrams 64
lattice model, of school curriculum 8
learning: assessment checks through 85; cognitive load theory and 66–7; conversations 26, 99, 118, 119–22, 125–7; cycle 45, 57–9; development of 45; disorders 50; environment within the classroom 80; episodes 25, 29, 131, 134; high-level planning 46; in the main 65–6; modality and the transient effect 68; outcomes 45; plenary 78; power to transform 66; quality of 83; redundancy effect 69; self-monitoring of 65; sequence of 71; split attention effect 67–8; techniques to develop 69–70; worked example effect 66–7
lessons: cycle 74; development of 46–9; planning 59; start of 59–65
life experiences 10, 37, 110
linear equations, solving of 21
linguistic knowledge 104
literacy skills 63; and cultural capital 103–5; development of 41–4, 104; impact on educational outcomes 103
literacy teaching 41
long-term memory 12, 25, 51, 53–5; development of students' 34; re-testing 98; schema construction for 53–5; storing information in 53; *see also* short-term memory; working memory
long-term plan *46*; composite knowledge 29
low-ability learners, support for 37

mastery, virtue of 48
mathematical calculation, process of *55*
mathematical equation 66, 72
mathematical sequence, development of 66
mathematics: high-level plan **23**; intent statement 17; literacy skills 17; opportunities to deepen understanding in *42*
medium-term plan 32, 44; composite knowledge 29; to deepen understanding 39–41; development of 34; subject-specific document 30

Index

memory 49–51; Atkinson–Shiffrin model of 51; episodic 51; long-term *see* long-term memory; of static information 52; types of 51–2; working 52–3
mental health 103, 110, 112
mission statement 6, 14
modelling, process of 71–3
multiple choice questions 87; key features of 87–8; from KS3 mathematics *88*

national curriculum 2, 4, 9–10, 27, 130; framework for 9; National Curriculum in England, The 9
National Literacy Trust 103
network curriculum 1, 8
non-linear curriculum models 8

OFSTED Framework (2019) 108, 118
open-ended tasks 64–5

pair matching activities 64, *65*
Paivio, Allan 56; dual-coding theory *57*
peer learning 124
penny-farthing, invention of 16
personal development 3; programme of 133
pillars, of the curriculum 9
powerful knowledge, concept of 10
prior knowledge 37; activation of *38*
problem-solving 71
procedural knowledge 31–2, 86–87; of adding fractions *33*
procedural memory 51
process-driven knowledge 47
professional development 45, 92, 95, 108, 115, 121, 125, 132

quality assurance 3, 27, 45, 117, 133; at every level within the school *120*; external 121; mass production phase 121; process of 121; through standardization and moderation 120
quality assurance cycle 7, 118–22
quality control 117–19, 128, 133

quality of inspector 121
question level analysis (QLA) 91–3; composite student level *93*; spreadsheet 97

redundancy effect 63, 66, 69, 71
reference point identification 50
reflective practitioners 120, 122
re-teach, policy of 93–99; dangers of 98
re-testing, in the case of a knowledge gap 98–9
retrieval practice 58, 63–4
revisiting knowledge 22–5; impact on retention *24*
right questions, selection of 87–9
rote-learning 48, 52

scaffolding: assessment 89–91; knowledge for 37–9, 71, 73–4, 130; quality of 124
schema construction 53, 55, 61
school curriculum 1; creation of 2; as learning tool 3; mission statement 6; quality assurance of 3; types of 8; values 6; vision statement 6
school values and ethos 1, 101
school vision 6–7, 14, 27, 80, 129, 134
science and mathematical subjects 8
semantic memory 52
SEND analysis 92, 120, 132
sensory filtering 50
sensory information, filtering of 49
sensory processing 49, 53
shared learning 10
short-term memory 51, 54; retrieval 63
social capital: development of 3, 104, 109–12; impact of learning 37; OFSTED reports on 109; targets for children 109; ways to enhance 112
social knowledge, impact on student' progress 101
social mobility, cycle of 103, 109–11
solving equations: concept of 5; 'I do' process for *72*; 'we do' process for *73*
spaced curriculum, concept of 25

Index

specific content knowledge, development of 18, 20, 22, 30
spiral curriculum 1, 8, 17, 26–7
split attention effect 67–8, 81
static information, memorization of 52
structural design, of school curriculum *9*
student books, quality of 117
student learning 48; conversations 125–7
subject and contextual knowledge *38*
subject intent statement *versus* high-level plan *23*
subject-specific vocabulary, teaching of 42
subject teams 7, 10, 99, 123, 127
subject vision, development of 7, 27, 129
substantive knowledge 31, 87
summary knowledge, in a computer science composite *89*
superficial learning 8
system of organization 54

taught knowledge 37
teacher: behaviour management 124; group analysis 92; planning, implications for 72
teaching: of Oliver Twist 37; quality of 91

threshold concepts: idea of 11–12; key characteristics of 11
'tick box' exercise 121
time management 78
transfer testing 98

Unequal Playing Field report 110–11

verbal associations 56
Victorian Britain 16, 19; knowledge of 37
Visible Learning Plus 48, 50, 111
vision statement 6
visual, auditory, kinaesthetic (VAK) 45
visual imagery 58
vocabulary tiers 106–7

whole year group analysis 94
worked example effect 68–9, 83
working memory 36, 50–6, 59, 66, 68–71, 73; impact of cognitive load on 47; limitations of 25, 39, 55; modelling 73–5; overloading of 65
written communication 44

Young, Michael 10

For Product Safety Concerns and Information please contact our EU
representative GPSR@taylorandfrancis.com
Taylor & Francis Verlag GmbH, Kaufingerstraße 24, 80331 München, Germany

www.ingramcontent.com/pod-product-compliance
Lightning Source LLC
Chambersburg PA
CBHW082212240426
43670CB00042B/2914